STOCK MARKETS
Comparative Analysis

The Author

Dr. B. J. Queensly Jeyanthi is as an Associate Professor of Commerce in the Research Centre of Commerce at Jayaraj Annapackiam College Autonomous, Periyakulam. She belongs to the congregation of sisters of St. Anne of Trichirappali. She has presented research papers in US and UK. She has published more than 30 papers in the reputed international journals and presented research papers in the national and international conferences and seminars. She has completed UGC sponsored minor and major project. She served as the Controller of Examinations for six years (2009 – 2015). She worked as the Head of the Department of Commerce with Computer Applications for eight years. She has published a book "A Study on National Stock Exchange of India". At present she is the Secretary of the College.

STOCK MARKETS
Comparative Analysis

– *Author* –

Dr. Sr. B.J. Queensly Jeyanthi

Secretary,
Jayaraj Annapackiam College for Women,
Periyakulam – 625 601
Tamil Nadu

2017

Scholars World

A Division of

Astral International Pvt. Ltd.

New Delhi – 110 002

ISBN 9789389605204 (Int. Edition)

Published by : **Scholars World**
A Division of
Astral International Pvt. Ltd.
– ISO 9001:2015 Certified Company –
4736/23, Ansari Road, Darya Ganj
New Delhi-110 002
Ph. 011-4354 9197, 2327 8134
E-mail: info@astralint.com
Website: www.astralint.com

Digitally Printed at : **Replika Press Pvt. Ltd.**

Acknowledgements

First and foremost I thank the lord Almighty for His showers of blessings for the successful completion of the Major Project. My Sincere thanks are due to Rev. Sr. Dr. T. Nirmala, M.Sc., B.Ed., Ph.D., DHRD, Principal and Rev. Sr. Dr. P.Helan Chandra, M.Sc., M.Phil., PGDCA., Ph.D., Secretary and our Superior Rev. Sr. Dr. Maria Alphonsal for their encouragement and support.

My sincere thanks are due to the UGC for supporting me with financial assistance. My sincere thanks are due to the faculty of the Department of Commerce with Computer Applications for their timely help. I remember all the hands which made this work a successful one.

Dr. Sr. B.J. Queensly Jeyanthi

Preface

The Financial system is the back bone of any economy in the modern world. The growth of an economy is largely influenced by financial markets—they allocate financial resources that are mobilised from savers and investors among users in the economy. The role of India's central bank, the Reserve Bank of India (RBI), in the development of financial markets in India is highly commendable. The stock market is witnessing its function in the development of the country and is increasingly gaining importance. The Indian stock exchanges have captured prominent place not only in Asia but also on at the global stage. The Bombay Stock Exchange (BSE) is one of the oldest exchanges across the world while the National Stock Exchange (NSE) is among the best in terms of sophistication and advancement of technology. After the implementation of the new economic policy in the early nineties, the Indian stock market really picked up. The Asian economies are advancing technology wise and are acting as an attraction for foreign capital. The increasing regionalization of economic activities and the liberalization of financial markets since the late 1980s resulted in regional economic integration, i.e., integration of the markets within the same region e.g. greater co-movement in the stock prices of South East Asian countries due to economic ties, lower geographical distance, and foreign investments or due to a common movement of fundamentals which is called the Contagion factor (Mukherjee and Mishra 2007)6.

The globalization of economic activity, the increased world wealth, and the reduction in transaction costs associated with the information revolution direct all the investors to consider the newly emerging financial markets. Interaction of financial markets is one of the most extensively discussed topics of financial literature. Various factors contributed to this dimension. These include cross -border movement of funds, the technological innovations in communications, scientific trading and settlement systems, and the introduction of innovative financial products. Globalizations also played a pivotal role in increase the interest in the study of dynamic inter-linkages among financial markets.

So this study is aimed to understand the dynamic inter-linkages between Indian stock exchange and the stock exchanges of developing and developed countries. If these markets are not integrated then benefits of portfolio diversification can be reaped by investors of these countries. Moreover, policy makers and regulators in these countries should not worry about any contagious effects. The study makes the comparative analysis of the Indian Stock Market with other international counterparts in respect of market efficiency, return, volatility and co-integration before and after the financial crisis. This book will help to understand the functions of stock exchange and it will be helpful to the investors to know the linkages between the stock markets.

In spite of the best efforts, it is possible that some errors may have occurred in the book. Further queries, constructive suggestions and criticisms for improvement of the book are always welcome and shall be thankfully acknowledged. Last but not the least, it is a pleasure for us to extend our sincere thanks to Mr. Anil Mittal, M/s Astral International Pvt. Ltd. and his team members for his keen interest shown in preparation and publishing of this book so efficiently and promptly.

Dr. Sr. B.J. Queensly Jeyanthi

Contents

List of Figures

List of Tables

Chapter 1
Introduction

1.1 Introduction

The Financial system is the back bone of any economy in the modern world. The Equity market is one of the important elements of this system. Ample evidence is available about the positive impact of stock market developments on economic growth (Levine and Zervos 1996[1]; Levine, 2002[2]; Nieuwerburgh *et al.*, 2006[3]; Enisan and Olufisayo 2009[4]).

The growth of an economy is largely influenced by financial markets—they allocate financial resources that are mobilised from savers and investors among users in the economy. The role of India's central bank, the Reserve Bank of India (RBI), in the development of financial markets in India is highly commendable. Market-determined interest and exchange rates, current account convertibility, monetary policy dealing with price-based instruments, auction-based allocation in the Government Securities Market (GSM), and phased capital account strengthened the financial system. Such a closely monitored development of the financial market is essential in an emerging and developing economy such as India to avoid financial instability, which is likely to occur otherwise (Gopinath, 2008)[5].

The stock market is witnessing its function in the development of the country and is increasingly gaining importance. The Indian stock exchanges have captured prominent place not only in Asia but also on at the global stage. The Bombay Stock Exchange (BSE) is one of the oldest exchanges across the world while the National Stock Exchange (NSE) is among the best in terms of sophistication and advancement of technology. After the implementation of the new economic policy in the early nineties, the Indian stock market really picked up. The dynamics of the world economy are changing. China and India happen to be the 2nd and the 4th largest economies respectively in the world in terms of GDP at purchasing power parity. The equity markets in emerging economies are on a high since 2005.

The Asian economies are advancing technology wise and are acting as an attraction for foreign capital. The increasing regionalization of economic activities and the liberalization of financial markets since the late 1980s resulted in regional economic integration, *i.e.*, integration of the markets within the same region *e.g.* greater co-movement in the stock prices of South East Asian countries due to economic ties, lower geographical distance, and foreign investments or due to a common movement of fundamentals which is called the *Contagion* factor (Mukherjee and Mishra 2007)[6].

During last two decades, globalization is the most visible feature in financial markets. Globalization tremendously changed the world in a new direction. In globally integrated financial markets, investors and policy makers are interested in taking advantage of efficiency enhancing aspects of market interaction. The Financial world is reshaping itself. Emerging equity markets are attracting the attention of global fund managers because these offer an opportunity for portfolio diversification. The benefits and costs of international portfolio diversification need to be considered by anyone holding a financial Portfolio. An efficient monitoring and controlling of this process of market interaction are necessary to avoid the undesirable destabilizing effects.

The globalization of economic activity, the increased world wealth, and the reduction in transaction costs associated with the information revolution direct all the investors to consider the newly emerging financial markets. Interaction of financial markets is one of the most extensively discussed topics of financial literature. Various factors contributed to this dimension. These include cross -border movement of funds, the technological innovations in communications, scientific trading and settlement systems, and the introduction of innovative financial products. Globalizations also played a pivotal role in increase the interest in the study of dynamic inter-linkages among financial markets.

So this study is aimed to understand the dynamic inter-linkages between Indian stock exchange and the stock exchanges of developing and developed countries. If these markets are not integrated then benefits of portfolio diversification can be reaped by investors of these countries. Moreover, policy makers and regulators in these countries should not worry about any contagious effects. The study makes the comparative analysis of the Indian Stock Market with other international counterparts in respect of market efficiency, return, volatility and co-integration before and after the financial crisis.

The recent global financial crisis has attracted the world in current periods. The global financial crisis caused by the sub-prime credit crisis in the US has destabilized the financial markets of the Asian countries. The financial crisis that swallows up the US during 2007-09 started with mortgage lending markets. The crisis has spread suddenly and strongly within the developed countries. The crisis has alarmed other developing countries and affected the significant economic progress. The purpose of this paper is to examine whether the Asian stock markets are interrelated after the financial crisis.

Nath and Verma (2003)[7] undertake a study of the long-run relationship between stock indices of India, Singapore and Taiwan. They applied bivariate and multivariate cointegration analysis and found no cointegration between those markets. It is worth noting that analyses above have been made in a normal context of economic and financial activities, so the results obtained at that time were reflecting the less integration of those marketplaces to the international financial sphere. This paper prompts to look at the change in behavior of major indices at the time of the 2008/2009 financial distress at the international level.

Sheng and Tu (2000)[8] have examined equity prices of Taiwan, Malaysia, Thailand, South-Korea, the Philippines, Indonesia, China, the U.S, Australia, Singapore, Japan and Hong-Kong before and during the period of 1998 Asian financial crisis. Daily closing price of respective stock exchange indices were collected from July 1, 1996 to June 30, 1999 and the multivariate Johansen cointegration test was run to provide evidence that supported the existence of the co-integrational relationship among the national stock indices during, but not before, the period of 1998 Asian financial crisis. They have asserted a strong relationship among South-East Asia and the leading role of the U.S market.

1.2 Problem Statement

The main aim of investors is to minimize the risk associated with their investment in stock. They have to find out the different portfolio for diversification benefits so that loss in one stock can be set off by income from another stock. This problem should be properly identified. Economic, political and natural calamities influence the stock markets and if these markets are co- integrated portfolio diversification benefits will be nullified. Some market may impact another market. Therefore, the current study is endeavoring to quantify and identify the impact of various Worldly Stock markets upon one another. The mutual interdependence of these markets will also be detected. It will work like a guiding star for the investors to diversify their national and international portfolios for investment. Globalisation is increasing at a fast pace and capital markets across the globe are getting integrated. Deregulation and market liberalisation measures, rapid development in the communication technology and computerised trading systems have accelerated the growth of Indian capital markets. India is one of the countries with expanding stock markets, increasingly attracting funds from FIIs.[9] The October 1987 global stock market crash, the Asian financial crisis during 1997–98 and the terrorist attacks on the US on 11th September 2001 affected the international markets. If the markets move together, then investing in various markets nullifies much of the gain arising out of diversification across the borders. The NSE has also attracted the attention of the global community as it has emerged as the third largest stock exchange in the world in terms of the number of transactions per day, next only to that of the NYSE and the NASDAQ. The average daily transactions that NSE logs today are in the range of 1.9 to 2.1 million trades.[10] Therefore, it is important for both investors and academicians to know whether stock markets are interrelated.

Hence, this study has been undertaken to analyse the market efficiency of the international stock markets, how Indian stock market differs from other stock markets in terms of return and volatility and whether Indian stock market is integrated with other stock markets.

1.3 Period of the Study

The empirical work is based on daily closing prices from April 1 2000 to March 31, 2015.To better analyze the relations between stock prices before and after Global Financial Crisis, the entire period is sub divided into two sub-periods and call the first sub-period which covered from 2000 April to 2007 July as pre-crisis period and the sub-period which covered from 2007 July to 2012 March as post-crisis period. The sample period choice was motivated by the fact that it's during the summer of 2007 the U.S. "subprime" crisis was spread to a number of other advanced economies through a combination of direct exposures to subprime assets, the gradual loss of confidence in a number of asset classes and the drying-up of wholesale financial markets. Hence, the year 2007 was taken for a standing point for analysis

1.4 Data

The empirical work is based on daily closing prices of the stock indices. Only secondary data were used. The data consisted of daily series of the S and P CNX Nifty (India), NASDAQ (USA), Nikkei (Japan), Hang–Seng (Hong Kong), TW11 (Taiwan) and STI (Singapore). Shanghai Composite (China) Jakarta Composite (Indonesia) KLSE Composite (Malaysia) Seoul Composite (South Korea) Australia (AORD), FTSE (UK), Dax(France) and CAC 40 (Germany). The data on daily stock markets indices were downloaded from the Yahoo Finance website (http://finance.yahoo.com).

1.4.1 Objectives of the Study

To test the weak form of Market efficiency of the stock markets of India and International Stock Markets.

To determine the volatility levels in the stock markets of India and International Stock Markets.

To draw a comparison between the Stock Markets of India and International Stock Markets important parameters like market capitalization, GDP, return and Volatility.

To examine cointegrationa and causality among Indian and International Markets.

1.5 Hypotheses

The Following null hypotheses have been formulated for testing.

- ☆ All the international stock markets are weak form efficient.
- ☆ Indian stock market is not cointegrated with other international markets.
- ☆ Indian stock market is not granger caused by the International Stock markets.

1.6 Methodology

1.6.1 Market Efficiency

To test the market efficiency, the study uses both traditional tests (such as, Kolmogorov Smirnov Goodness of Fit, run test, autocorrelation test and Ljung Box test) and dynamic time series model Dickey–Fuller Test (Unit Root) and Augmented Dickey–Fuller (ADF) test. The following formulas are used for that.

A. Kolmogorov Smirnov Goodness of Fit Test

Kolmogorov Smirnov Goodness of Fit Test (KS) is a non –parametric test and is used to determine how well a random sample of data fits a particular distribution (normal). It is based on comparison of the sample's cumulative distribution against the standard cumulative function for each distribution and test whether the distribution are homogeneous. We use normal parameters to test distribution.

The Kolmogorov-Smirnov test statistic is defined as[11]

$$D = \max_{1 \le i \le N} \left(F(Y_i) - \frac{i-1}{N}, \frac{i}{N} - F(Y_i) \right)$$

where F is the theoretical cumulative distribution of the distribution being tested which must be a continuous distribution (*i.e.*, no discrete distributions such as the binomial or Poisson), and it must be fully specified (*i.e.*, the location, scale, and shape parameters cannot be estimated from the data). The calculated value of Z is compared with a critical value of a Z in the One –Sample Kolmogorov Goodness –of –Fit Test table for a given sample size [12].

Our hypothesis for this test is shown as the following;

H_0: The data follow a normal distribution

H_a: The data do not follow the normal distribution

B. The Runs Analysis

The run test is another approach to detect the statistical independencies which means randomness. A run is a sequence of consecutive positive or negative returns. By comparing the total number of runs in the data with the expected number of runs under random walk hypothesis, the test of the random walk hypothesis may be constructed. To perform the test, the sampling distribution of the total number of runs in a sample is required. The r –statistic follows a normal distribution with a mean and standard deviation given by the following formulae. [13]

$$\mu(r_i) = 2n_1n_2/(n_1+n_2)+1$$

$$\sigma(r_i) = \sqrt{2n_1n_2(2n_1n_2 - n_1n_2)/(n_1+n_2)^2(n_1+n_2-1)}$$

This test is performed by examining a time series of returns for a security and testing whether the number of consecutive price gains or drops shows a pattern. A price gain is represented by a " +", a price drop is represented by a "- " and "0" shows that return is zero. The run test converts the total number of runs into a Z statistic. For large samples the Z statistics gives the probability of difference between actual and expected number of runs. The Z values is greater than or equal to 1.96, then the null hypothesis that stock returns follow random walk is rejected. The null hypothesis is that stock returns depict a random walk through time. If the absolute value of Z is greater than Z critical value 1.96 for =0.05)

Our hypothesis for run test shown as the following;

H0: Price changes are random.

H1: Price changes are not random.

C. Autocorrelation Test ACF(k)

The autocorrelation coefficient provides a measure of the relationship between the value of a random variable in time t (x_t) and its value at k periods earlier (x_{t-k}). This indicates whether price changes at time t are influenced by price changes occurring at k periods earlier. The autocorrelation function ACF(k) for the time series Y_t and the k–lagged series Y_{t-k} is defined as:[14]

$$ACF(k) = \frac{\sum_{t=k+1}^{n}(Y_t - \overline{Y})(Y_{t-k} - \overline{Y})}{\sum_{t=1}^{n}(Y_t - \overline{Y})^2}$$

Where $\overline{Y}$ is the overall mean of the series with n observations.

The standard error of ACF (k) is given by:

$^{Se}ACF\ (k) = 1/\sqrt{n-k}$

When n is sufficiently large (n > 50), the approximate value of the standard error of ACF(k) is given by[15] :

$$^{Se}\ ACF\ (k) = \sqrt{\frac{1+2\sum_{i=1}^{k-1} r_i^{\,2}}{n}}$$

where

r_i = Autocorrelation at lag i

k = The time lag

n = Number of observations in the data series

To test whether ACF (k) are significantly different from zero, the following distribution of t is used:

$t = ACF(k)\ /\ Se_{ACF(k)}$

D. Ljung–Box Statistic

Ljung–Box (LB) statistic is used to test the joint hypothesis that all the autocorrelations for lag one through m are simultaneously equal to zero. The value of the LB statistic is compared with the chi-square table to assess if it is significant.

Ljung–Box statistic, is defined as[16]

$$LB = n(n+2)\sum_{k=1}^{m}\left(\frac{r_k^{\,2}}{n-k}\right) \approx \chi^2 m$$

The LB statistic follows the chi-square distribution with m (the number of time lags to be tested) degrees of freedom. The null hypothesis is that all r_k are zero. If the computed LB exceeds the critical LB value from the chi-square table at the chosen level of significance, the null hypothesis is rejected. In such a situation, the result suggests dependency of the series, which violates the assumption of market efficiency. The chi-square value for fourteen degrees of freedom at 5 per cent level of significance is 24.99.

E. Augmented Dickey–Fuller Test (Unit Root)

The Dickey–Fuller statistic applies only to an autoregression (1) model. For some series autoregression (1) model does not capture all the serial correlation in (y_t). In Dickey–Fuller test it is assumed that the white noise error term is uncorrelated. Dickey and Fuller have developed a higher order autoregression, the Augmented Dickey–Fuller (ADF) test, in case μ_t are correlated.

The Augmented Dickey–Fuller (ADF) test is estimated by the following formula: [17]

$$\Delta Y_t = \beta_1 + \beta_2 t + \delta Y_{t-1} + \alpha_i \sum_{i=1}^{m} \Delta Y_{t-i} + \mu_t$$

Where μ_t is a white noise error term and $\Delta Y_{t-1} = (Y_{t-1} - Y_{t-2})$. The null hypothesis $H_0: \delta = 0$, and the alternative hypothesis $H_1: \delta < 0$.The critical value of ADF test at 5 per cent level of significance is –3.41.

1.6.2 Volatility

Close to close volatility, open to open volatility, open close volatility and high low volatility models are used to calculate volatility. ARCH and GARCH model is used to capture volatility transmission.

Return is calculated using logarithmic method as follows.

$r_t = (\log p_t - \log p_{t-1})*100$

A. Inter-day Volatility

The variation in share price return between the two trading days is called inter-day volatility. Inter-day volatility is computed by close to close and open to open value of any index level on a daily basis. Standard deviation is used to calculate inter-day volatility.

B. Close to Close Volatility

Close to close volatility (standard estimation volatility) is measured with the following formula:

$$\sigma = \sqrt{(1/n-1)\sum(r_t - \bar{r})^2}$$

C. Open to Open Volatility

Open to open volatility is considered necessary for many market participants because opening prices of shares and the index value reflect any positive or negative information that arrives after the close of the market and before the start of the next day's trading.The following formula is used to calculate open-to-open volatility:[18]

$$\sigma = \sqrt{(1/n-1)\sum(r_t - \bar{r})^2}$$

Inter-day volatility takes into account only close to close and open to open index value and it is measured by standard deviation of returns.

D. Intra-day Volatility

The variation in share price return within the trading day is called intra-day volatility. It indicates how the indices and shares behave in a particular day. Intra-day volatility is calculated with the help of Parkinson Model and Garman and Klass model.

E. Parkinson Model

High-low volatility is calculated with the following formula:[19]

$$\sigma = k\sqrt{1/n\sum \log(H_t / L_t)^2}$$

F. Garman and Klass Model

The Garman and Klass model is used to calculate the open–close volatility. The formula for Garman and Klass model (1980) takes the following form.[20]

$$\sigma = \sqrt{1/n\sum(1/2)[\log(H_t / L_t)]^2 - [2\log(2)-1][\log(C_t / O_t)]^2}$$

Engle Granger Dickey–Fuller test for cointegration EG–DF (Engle–Granger 1987), The Engle Granger Augmented Dickey–Fuller test and Granger Causality test is used to examine the short run between the stock markets.

1.6.3 Cointegration

Before conducting cointegration test it is of interesting to determine if there are any common forces driving the long-run movement of the data series or if each individual stock index is driven solely by its own fundamentals. Cointegration analysis is used to investigate long term relationship between Indian and other International stock markets and it is estimated by ordinary least squares under the following formula:[21]

$$X_t = \beta_1 + \delta Y_t + \mu_t$$

The Engle Granger Augmented Dickey–Fuller test is applied on the 'cointegrtating residuals' μ_t obtained from the equation (1). The formula for EG–ADF test is as follows[22]

$$\Delta\mu_t = -\delta\mu_{t-1} + a_i \sum_{i=1}^{m} \Delta\mu_{t-1} + \mu_t$$

$\Delta\mu_t$ represents the first differences of the residuals The specific hypotheses are :

$H_0 : \delta = 0$

$H_1 : \delta \neq 0$

Null hypothesis is that there is no co integration among the stock indices. The value of a calculated absolute tau (τ) value is greater than the tabulated critical (τ) value; the null hypothesis of no cointegration is rejected. Engle and Granger have provided the critical values of ADF statistics.

1.6.4 Granger Causality

Short run integration is examined using Granger's (1969) causality test. Formally, a time series x_t Granger – causes another time series y_t if series y_t can be predicted with better accuracy by using past values of x_t rather than by not doing so, other information being identical. In other words, variable x_t fails Granger –cause y_t if

$$\Pr(y_{t+m} \mid \Omega_t) = \Pr(y_{t+m} \mid \Psi_t),$$

Where Pr (y_{t+m} | $\grave{U}_t$) denotes conditional probability of y_t, Ω_t is the set of all information available at time t, and Pr(y_{t+m} | Ψ_t) denotes conditional probability of y_t obtained by excluding all information on x_t from y_t this set of information is depicted as Ψ_t. To examine the causality, if a cointegration relationship is found, a Vector Error Correction Model (VECM) is estimated.[23]

$$x_t = \alpha_0 + \sum_{j=1}^{k} \gamma_j x_{t-j} + \sum_{j=1}^{k} \beta_j y_{t-j} + \mu_{xt}$$

$$y_t = \alpha_0 + \sum_{j=1}^{k} \gamma_j x_{t-j} + \sum_{j=1}^{k} \beta_j y_{t-j} + \mu_{yt}$$

where ε_{t-1} represents the deviation from long-run equilibrium in period t-1 obtained from the cointegration regression. Where k is a suitably chosen positive integer, γ_j and β_j, j = 0,1 ......k are parameters and α' are constants and μ_t's are disturbance terms with zero means and finite variances. The null hypothesis that y_t does not Granger – cause x_t is not accepted if the β_j's, j>0 in equation (4) are jointly significantly different from zero using a standard joint test (*e.g.*, and F test). Similarly, x_t Granger – causes y_t, if the λ_j's j >0 coefficients in equation (5) are jointly different from zero. For non -cointegrating series, Granger causality is examined by the Vector Autoregressive (VAR) model. The form of the VAR model is obtained by deleting the ε_{t-1} terms in (4) and (5).

The stationary series are also cross – correlated. The cross - correlation between the time series are tested by using the following formula:[24]

$$\gamma_{x_y\ y_t}(k) = \frac{\sum_{t=1}^{T-K}(x_t - \bar{x})(y_{t+k} - \bar{y})}{\left[\sum_{t=1}^{T}(x_t - \bar{x})^2 \sum_{t=1}^{T}(y_t - \bar{y})^2\right]^{1/2}}$$

Where k is greater than, equal to, or less than zero.

The significance of estimated cross – correlation is assessed by using approximate standard error, $T^{-½}$, (Bartlet, 1966), of the sample of cross – correlation. This helps to identify the causality patterns associated with, $\gamma x_t\, y_t(k)$. This method was used, among others, by Ahmad (1989) in estimating the cross – correlations between two interest rate series.

1.7 Structure of the Study

Chapter two reviews most of the literature related to market efficiency, volatility and stock market integration.

Chapter three presents the review of general features of all the stock markets at the same time it discusses the main macroeconomic indicators for these countries.

Chapter four analyses the efficiency of the markets and how the market is efficient before and after the financial crisis.

Chapter five explains the returns and stock market volatility at different periods. That is before and after the financial crisis.

Chapter six empirically estimates the integration among the stock markets between Indian and other developing and developed stock markets. The study uses the recently developed Engle Granger Dickey Fuller Model for capturing long run relationship between the stock markets. More over this chapter estimates the Granger Causality among the stock markets.

Chapter seven summarises conclusions derived through this study. This chapter presents the summary of the previous chapters and discuss the policy implications of the major chapters. Finally suggestions for the future work are provided at the end of the chapter.

References

1. Levine, Ross, and Zervos, Sara (1996a)." Stock Market Development and Long-Run Growth", **The World Bank, Policy Research Working Paper** No. 1582.
2. Levine, Ross, and Zervos, Sara (2002), Stock Markets, Banks, **and** Economic Growth P The World Bank **Policy Research Working Paper No:** 1690,

3. Nieuwerburgh, *et al.* (2006), "Stock Market and Economic Growth in Belgium", **Explorations in Economic History,** 43 (1), 13-38,

4. Enisan, A.A. and Olufisayo (2009), "Stock Market Development and Economic Growth: Evidence from Seven Sub - Sahara African Countries". **J Econ Bus** 61: 162 - 171.

5. Mukherjee and Mishra, (2007), "International Stock Market and Its Economic Determinants: A study of Indian and World Equity Markets", **Vikalpa,** VOL 32, No 4. 8.

6. Gopinath (2008), "Frequency of price adjustment and pass-through" **National Bureau of Economic Research**

7. Nath, G.C. and S. Verma, (2003) "Study of common stochastic trend and co-integration in the emerging markets: A case study of India, Singapore and Taiwan". **NSE Research Paper** No.72, National Stock Exchange, Mumbai, India.

8. Sheng H., Tu A. (2000). "A Study of Co-integration and Variance Decomposition Among National Equity Indices Before and During the Period of the Asian Financial Crisis". **Journal of Multi-international Financial Management** 10(3-4), 345-365.

9. Patil, R.H., "NSE:Clicking on with Investors", **The Hindu Business Line,** 28thJanuary2004. www.blonet.com/bI10/stories/2004012800461200. htm

10. Damodar, N.Gujarati, **Basic Econometrics**, Tata McGraw–Hill Publishing Company Limited, New Delhi, 2004, p.799.

11. NSDL Annual Report, 2001–2002, p.5.

12. Kiran Kumar, "Equity Market Linkages–A Case of US and India", **NSE News**, November 2002, p.3.

13. Patil, R.H., "NSE:Clicking on with Investors", **The Hindu Business Line,** 28thJanuary2004. www.blonet.com/bI10/stories/2004012800461200. htm

14. Damodar, N.Gujarati, **Basic Econometrics**, Tata McGraw–Hill Publishing Company Limited, New Delhi, 2004, p.799.

15. http://www.itl.nist.gov/div898/handbook/eda/section3/eda35g.htm

16. Oktay Tas_ Salim Dursunoglu (2005), "Testing Random Walk Hypothesis for Istanbul Stock exchange" http://services.bepress.com/itfa/15th/art38

17. Vaidyanathan and Gandhi Kumar Gali (1994), Efficiency of the Indian Capital Market" **Indian Journal of Finance and Research** Vol 5,No.2, PP 27 – 40.

18. Kendall, M.G., "The Analysis of Economic Time Series–Part I Prices", **Journal of Royal Statistical Society**, Series A (General), 1953, Vol. 116, Pt. 1, ii- 25, Reprinted in Cootner, 1964, pp.85–99.

19. John, E. Hanke, Arthur, G. Reitsch and Dean W. Wichern, **Business Forecasting**, Prentice Hall of India, Private Limited, New Delhi, 2002, p.57.

20. Ljung, G.M. and G.P.E. Box, "On a Measure of Lack of Fit in Time Series Models", **Biometrika**, Vol.65, No.2, 1978, pp.297–303.

21. James, H. Stock and Mark, W. Watson, **Introduction to Econometrics**, Pearson Education Ltd, Delhi, 2004, p.462.

22. Euro monitor 2010, Appendix

23. Granger C W J (1969), "Investigating Causal Relations by Econometric Models and Cross Spectral Methods", *Econometrica,* Vol. 37, No. 3, pp. 424-438.

Chapter 2

Review of Literature

2.1 Introduction

Market efficiency is an essential feature of any financial market. It has an influence on the investment strategy of an investor, if market is efficient, trying to pick up winners will be a waste of time. Informational efficiency of financial markets has attracted much attention among financial scholars and practitioners. The issues are important to security analysts, investors and security exchange regulatory bodies in their policy making decisions to improve the market condition. The macro economic event that takes place nationally and internationally leads to volatility in stock prices apart from company specific factors. Volatility in the stock price affects the returns of the investors. The globalisation of securities market has brought an increased attention to stock markets throughout the world. If stock markets move together the market absorbs the shocks of other markets and nullifies the portfolio diversification benefits. Therefore, it is important for both investors and academicians to know whether stock markets are interlinked. The issue is also important for policy makers to prevent the spill over effect. The pre-eminent positions of the stock market in the national economy, the growth in the investor base and the globalisation have induced the researcher to study the market efficiency, volatility and cointegration. Studies related to these aspects of stock markets were dated back to 1965, Fama (1965)[1], Grubel (1968),[2] Conard and Juttner (1973),[3],Bruno H. Solnik (1973),[4] Agmon T (1974),[5] James C. Dyer (1976),[6] Paul Barnes (1986),[7] Andrew W. Lo and A.C. Mackinlay (1988),[8] Skinner. D.J (1989),[9] Taylor and Tonks (1989),[10] Rao and Naik (1990),[11] Schwart G.W. (1990),[12] Larry J. Lockwood and Scott C. Linn (1990),[13] Theodore E. Day and Craig M. Lewis (1992),[14] Kam C. Chan, Benton E. Gup and Ming-Shiun Pan (1992),[15] Kasa (1992),[16] Richard Roll (1992)[17] Dickinson and Muragu (1994)[18]

This chapter concerns with review of important empirical works, concerning stock market efficiency, stock market volatility and stock market integration starting from 2000 to 2015. The review of literature is undertaken in three sections. The first section focuses on the review of empirical works related to market efficiency. Similarly, the second section deals with the review of studies concerned with stock market volatility and finally third section deals with the review of studies pertaining to stock market integration. But studies from the year 2000 are taken for review.

2.2 Studies Relating to Market Efficiency

Ramasastri A.S. (2000)[19] analysed the efficiency of the Indian stock market from 1991 to 1998 on the daily data on Sensex. He employed unit root test and concluded that the Indian stock markets were efficient during the study period

Asma Mobarek and Kevin Keasey, (2000)[20] scrutinised the weak form efficiency of Dhaka Stock Exchange using daily market returns of the Dhaka Stock Exchange for a period from January, 1988 to December, 1997. He employed Non-parametric test that is run test, Kolmogrov Smirnov Goodness of fit test and parametric test namely autocorrelation, autoregressive and ARIMA and concluded that the Dhaka Stock Exchange of Bangladesh was not efficient at weak form.

Hyun-Jung Ryoo and Graham Smith (2000)[21] tested the random walk hypothesis for the Korean stock market over a period from March, 1988 to December, 1998. During that time there were five regimes of daily price limits. They used a sample of 55 actively traded stocks to cover a wide range of industries with a marked number of limit moves and tested the random walk hypothesis under each price limit regime. They concluded that the system of price limits prevented a random walk process and the market was inefficient. As the daily price limits were increased, the proportion of stock prices following a random walk also increased. That is, the stock market as a whole approached a random walk as price limits were relaxed.

Sarath P. Abeysekera (2001)[22] examined the behaviour of stock returns on the Colombo Stock Exchange (CSE) with a view to determine its consistency with the weak form of the Efficient Market Hypothesis. They employed daily, weekly and monthly returns of stock indices for a period from January, 1991 to November, 1996. They used the Sensitive Share Price Index (SSI) and a forty-security value weighted index adjusted for dividends, splits, rights and bonuses. Results of the study indicated that the stocks traded in CSE did not behave in a consistent manner with the weak form of the Efficient Market Hypothesis.

Ramasastri A.S (2001)[23] carried out an analysis to study the three phases of Indian stock markets in the nineties. Daily data pertaining to BSE Sensex and nine companies from January, 1991 to December, 1999 were used for the study. He identified three phases namely, turbulent phase (1991–92), transition phase (1993) and transformed phase (1996–99). Market efficiency was tested by runs test and variance ratio tests. Relative efficiency was tested by average run length and variance ratios graph. According to runs test, market was efficient during the turbulence phase but not during the transition phase and the transformed phase. Average run length and relative variance ratios graph showed that markets in the transformed phase was more efficient than they were in transition phase and concluded that changes brought into the functioning of stock exchanges due to IT innovations,

SEBI guidelines and FIIs participation had a positive impact on market efficiency in the Indian context.

Pradhan H.K. and Lakshmi S. Narasimhan (2002)[24] investigated the behaviour of Indian stock price indices for 12 years from 1990 to 2001. The study was based upon three Indian stock market indices namely BSE–30, BSE–100 and S and P CNX Nifty. Various tests of market efficiency suggested that the Indian stock market was growing informationally efficient and efficiency had increased over the time. The volatility of the returns was found to increase over the period under study and this could be partly attributed to the impact of foreign portfolio flows. Also there was significant asymmetric volatility that is negative news had more impact on the variance of the returns than positive news. Granger Causality tests suggested that domestic returns affected foreign portfolio flows and, in turn, affected domestic returns and its variance.

Chandra Babu and Punithavathy Pandian (2002)[25] investigated the weak form efficiency of the Indian stock market. They used daily and weekly closing stock prices of 40 companies from different industries and six leading indices namely the BSE 200, the BSE Sensex, the S and P CNX 500, the CNX Defty, the S and P CNX Nifty and the CNX Nifty Junior from 1995 to January 2001. They applied autocorrelation test, runs test and concluded that Indian stock market was not weak form efficient.

Sunil Poshakwale (2002)[26] examined the random walk hypothesis for the emerging Indian stock market by using daily returns calculated from an equally weighted portfolio of 100 stocks and a sample of 38 most actively traded stocks in the Bombay Stock Exchange from 1st January, 1990 to 30th November, 1998. The study report rejected the random walk model of efficient price formation for the Indian market.

Chaudhuri and Wu (2003)[27] investigated whether stock price indexes of emerging markets can be characterized as random walk (unit root) or mean reversion processes. Applying a panel based test for 17 emerging equity markets during the period from January 1985 to April 2002. The results rejected the null hypothesis of random walk in favour of mean reversion at the 5 percent significance level.

Hasan (2004)[28] examined the random walk hypothesis using the daily data of the Dhaka Stock Exchange. The estimated results showed that the null hypothesis of randomness cannot be rejected and stock prices had a significant random walk or permanent component.

Oktay Tas and Salim Dursunaglu (2005)[29] studied the weak form market efficiency of Istanbul Stock Exchange. ISE National-30 index companies from January, 1995 to January, 2004 were used for the study. Istanbul stock exchange's daily stock returns were used for testing the Random Walk Hypothesis and Efficient Market Hypothesis. They used Dickey-Fuller unit root test and runs test; both the tests rejected the efficient market hypothesis and concluded that ISE was inefficient.

Natalia Abrosimova Deloitte and Gishan Dissanaike (2005)[30] examined the existence of weak-form efficiency in the Russian stock market during the period from 1st September 1995 to 1st May 2001 using daily, weekly and monthly Russian Trading System index time series. Unit root, autocorrelation and variance ratio tests were conducted for the null hypothesis of a random walk model. The results supported the null hypothesis for the monthly data only. Their research results provided some limited evidence of short-term market predictability on the Russian stock market.

Lean and Smyth (2007)[31] examined the random walk hypothesis for stock prices in eight Asian countries by applying univariate and panel Lagrange Multiplier (LM) unit root tests with one and two structural breaks. The results from the univariate LM unit root tests and panel LM unit root test with one structural break suggested that stock prices in each country was characterized by a random walk, but the findings from the panel LM unit root test with two structural breaks suggested that stock prices in the eight countries were mean reverting.

Rakesh Gupta and Parikshit K. Basu (2007)[32] tested the weak form efficiency in the framework of random walk hypothesis for the BSE and NSE equity markets in India for the period from 1991 to 2006. The evidence suggested that the series did not follow random walk model and there was an evidence of autocorrelation in both markets rejecting the weak form efficiency hypothesis.

Purna Chandra Padhan (2009)[33] examined random walk hypothesis in the different categories of Bombay Stock Exchange (BSE) Mumbai. The data for 33 firms were considered across various industries. The daily adjusted closing stock prices of these companies were gathered since April 1990 to Feb 15, 2007. The study found sufficient evidence that stock prices of various firms supported random walk hypothesis during the study period and concluded that, it is practically difficult to predict the stock price based on past observations. Stock price follows random walk process mainly due to firm specific factors apart from economic and financial factors.

Ibrahim Awad and Zahran Daraghma (2009)[34] examined the efficiency of the Palestine Security Exchange (PSE) at the weak-level for 35 stocks listed in the market by using daily observations of the PSE indices: Alquds index, general index, and sector indices. Parametric and nonparametric tests for examining the randomness of the PSE stock prices were utilized. The study utilized nonparametric tests for investigating the efficiency of the PSE at the weak level, especially, the results of Jarque-Bera test for normality showed that the daily returns of the PSE are not normally distributed. The serial correlation tests and the runs tests both revealed that the daily returns are inefficient at the weak-form. Also, the unit root tests (Augmented Dickey-Fuller (ADF) unit root test and Phillips-Peron (PP) unit root test) suggest the weak-form inefficiency in the return series. However, the PSE is inefficient at the weak level; as a result, this is likely to be an evidence that the prudent investor who deals with the PSE will achieve abnormal returns using historical data of stock prices, and trading volume.

2.3 Studies Related to Stock Market Volatility

Daniel G. Weaver (2002)[35] examined the differences in intra day volatility between stock trading on the NYSE and the NASDAQ, under the stable as well as the stressful market conditions during 2001. The data consisted of CBOE and AMEX option listings from April 1973 to December 1986. He concluded that the NYSE stocks exhibited consistently lower intra-day volatility than the NASDAQ stocks. Simple standard deviation of return, standard deviation of continuously compounded returns and the average of squared returns were used for analysis. They suggested that a specialised market structure was associated with lower volatility.

Thenmozhi M. (2002)[36] made an attempt to determine if there was any change in the volatility of the underlying index due to the introduction of Nifty futures and whether movements in the futures price provided predictive information regarding subsequent movements in the index prices. Daily closing price returns of the S and P CNX Nifty were considered from 15th June, 1998 to 26th July, 2002. The results revealed that the information flow was higher in the post futures period and resulted in a decline in spot index volatility in the post futures period. It was found that futures market transmitted information to cash market and futures market was faster than spot market in processing information. The analysis done for different time periods reinforced that the futures market tended to lead the spot market and the index futures market served as a price discovery vehicle for stock prices.

Samanta G.P. (2003)[37] analysed the link between stock market volatility, excess returns and future output growth. He applied autoregressive model. The S and P CNX Nifty was chosen from April 1993 to December 2002. The result proved that stock market volatility was strongly influenced by its own past values. The volatility was also quite strongly related (at least contemporaneously) to excess returns in recent years.

Golaka C. Nath (2003)[38] studied the behaviour of volatility in cash market after the introduction of derivatives. The S and P CNX Nifty and the CNX Nifty Junior and 20 stocks were selected randomly from the S and P CNX Nifty and the CNX Nifty Junior index for studying the volatility behavior during the period January, 1999 to October, 2003. They classified the entire period into five time buckets, taking into account after the introduction of futures on individual stocks and indices options on individual stocks and indices by considering the last time buckets from November, 2002 to October, 2003. They used 4 different methods GARCH (1, 1), IGARCH with $\lambda = 0.94$, one year rolling window of standard deviation and a 6 month rolling standard deviation. They concluded that the volatility of the market fell in the post derivative period.

George C. Pardee (2003)[39] examined the stock market volatility of 12 developed countries. The monthly returns were calculated for each of those countries from the late 19th or early 20th century to 2002 from their starting date of trading. They established that volatility had not been constant. There was an evidence of u-shaped pattern of volatility in majority of the countries. To explain these u-shaped trends they examined the role of monetary policy and financial internationalisation, found a positive association of monetary volatility with stock market volatility and suggested that the conduct of monetary regime was important for stock market volatility. They further found that financial internationalization was also positively associated with stock market volatility.

Charles P. Johnson, Mark D. William and Jack W. Wilson (2004)[40] developed a simple measure of volatility based on extreme day returns and applied it to market returns from 1885 to 2002 on S and P 500 index and DJIA for a period of 18 years. They proved that extreme returns are a better measure of stock market risk than the traditional standard deviation. They exhibited that volatility changed from 1885 to 2002 with no secular trend, that there was some persistence in volatility and the volatility was higher in bear markets than in bull markets.

Raju Anirban Ghosh M.T. (2004)[41] compared the international stock market volatility among six developed markets namely, the USA, the UK, France, Germany, Australia, Hong Kong and the twelve emerging markets namely India, Singapore, Malaysia, China, Indonesia, Chile, Brazil, Mexico, South Africa, Korea and Taiwan using daily closing index price of 24 year period from January 1980 to December 2003. They used Parkinson (1980) model, Garman and Klass (1980) model, open to open volatility model and traditional close-to-close volatility model. They arrived at the conclusion that many of the developed and all emerging markets experienced high volatility from 1997 to 2002 indicating convergence of markets. Volatility was low in 2003 in almost all the countries compared to emerging markets and some of the developed markets. India experienced a low intra-day volatility. Extreme value volatility in India touched its peak in 2000 at 3.17 per cent and continuously slided thereafter.

Julan Du and Shang–Jin Wei (2004)[42] studied whether insider trading contributed to a rise in market volatility across countries. They used the average of the ratings in 1977 and 1998 for measuring insider trading. They evidenced that more insider trading was found to be associated with a higher market volatility even after one controls for the volatility of the real output growth, volatility of monetary and fiscal policies and maturity of the stock market. Moreover, the quantitative effect of insider trading on market volatility was also big when compared with the effect of the volatility of other fundamentals.

Parthapratim Pal (2004)[43] analysed the volatility of Indian stock markets and the behavior of Foreign Institutional Investors in India.Data from BSE Sensex for a period of March 2004 to June 2004 were taken for the study and further he analysed how the withdrawal of foreign portfolio capital in the post election phase affected the price and equity holding pattern of different Sensex companies. The result of the study showed that not only the FIIs were the major players in the domestic stock market in India but their influence on the domestic market was also growing. After the general election in India the sudden reversal of FIIs flows triggered a panic reaction which resulted in very high volatility in the Indian stock market.

Lieven Baele (2004)[44] analysed the volatility spillover effects in European stock markets using weekly total (dividend-adjusted) continuously compounded stock returns from 8 EMU countries (Austria, Belgium, France, Germany, Ireland, Italy, the Netherlands, and Spain), three European Union (EU) countries that do not participate in EMU (Denmark, Sweden, and the UK), two countries from outside the EU (Norway, and Switzerland), and two regional markets (the aggregate European markets, and the US. The data covered the period of January 1980 - August 2001. He found that both the EU and US volatility spillover intensity had increased over the 1980s and 1990s, the rise was more pronounced for EU spillovers. In most countries, shock spillover intensities increased most strongly in the second half of 1980s and the first half of the 1990s. Increased trade integration, equity market development, and low inflation had contributed to the increase in EU shock spillover intensity.

Madhusudanan Karmakar (2005)[45] estimated conditional volatility models in an effort to capture the salient features of stock market volatility in India and evaluated the models in terms of out-of-sample forecast accuracy; he also investigated whether there was any leverage effect in Indian companies. The estimation of volatility was made at macro level on two major market indices, namely S and P CNX Nifty and BSE Sensex from 2nd January, 1991 to 10th June, 2003. GARCH (1, 1) model was fitted to both the market indices. They found strong evidence of time-varying volatility and a tendency of the periods of high and low volatility to cluster, a higher persistence and predictability of volatility and they concluded that the various GARCH models provided good forecasts of volatility and are useful for portfolio allocation, performance measurement, option valuation etc.

Golaka C Nath and Manoj Dalvi (2005)[46] computed various kinds of volatility measures and studied their relative performance using simple statistical methods. The S and P CNX Nifty daily prices from January, 1999 to December 2003 were taken for the study. They concluded that the realised volatility estimates using the sum of squared returns from high frequency data performed better than the usual GARCH models. The result was in agreement with the findings of developed markets.

Ajay Pandey (2005)[47] evaluated the extreme value volatility estimators and their empirical performance in Indian capital market. He used the S and P CNX Nifty data from January 1999 to December 2002 and used two traditional estimators (close to close volatility and mean adjusted version of the close to close estimation), four extreme value estimators (Parkinson, Garman and Klass, Rogers Satchell and Yang–Zhang) and two conditional volatility models GARCH (1, 1) model and E GARCH model volatility. According to him, for estimating the volatility, the extreme value estimators perform better on efficiency criteria than the conditional models. Conditional volatility models performed better than the extreme value estimators in respect of bias.

Siong Hook Law (2006)[48] investigated whether stock return volatility has returned to pre-financial crisis levels (Asian Financial crisis), using the Exponential GARCH model combined with sudden changes of unconditional variance. The empirical results indicated that the KLSE had protracted stock market volatility after the Asian financial crisis. In March 2003, stock return volatility in the KLSE was decreasing, but had still not returned to pre-financial crisis levels and identified high volatility during the period from 1985 to 2003, namely: (i) the stock market crash of October 1987; (ii) when Iraq invaded Kuwait in August 1990; and (iii) the sudden and massive capital flight of early 1994.

Frimpong Joseph and Oteng-Abayie (2006)[49] studied the dynamics of the Ghana stock market volatility over a period of 10 years. The daily closing prices of the Ghana Stock Exchange Databank Stock Index (DSI) from 15 June 1994 to 28 April 2004 were used for the study. They found that the DSI exhibited the stylised characteristics such as volatility clustering, leptokurtosis and asymmetry effects associated with stock returns on more advanced stock markets. The random walk hypothesis was also rejected for the GSE DSI returns.

Rajni Mala and Mahendra Reddy (2007)[50] examined the presence of the stock market volatility on Fiji's stock market using the Autoregressive Conditional Heteroskedasticity (ARCH) models and the Generalized ARCH model. The analysis was done using a time series data for the period 2001- 2005 on specific firms and it was found out that seven out of the sixteen firms listed on Fiji's stock market was volatile further it confirmed that the interest rates changes had a significant effect on stock market volatility.

J. Cunado, Gil-Alana and Perez de Gracia (2008)[51], tested whether the stock market volatility presented a different behavior in bull and bear phases. They estimated the order of integration in the squared returns in the US stock market (S and P 500) using long range dependence techniques over the sample period from August, 1928 to December, 2006. The results suggested that squared returns presented long memory behavior. The results also showed that in many cases the volatility was more persistent in the bear market than in the bull market.

Lucía de las Nieves Morales (2008)[52], investigated the nature of volatility spillovers between stock returns and a number of exchange rates in six Latin American countries and one European economy in the 1998-2006 period. The results showed that the volatility of stock returns affected the volatility of exchange rates; however, no evidence of volatility transmission in the opposite direction was found.

T. Mallikarjunappa1 and Afsal E. M **(2008)**[53] studied the volatility implications of the introduction of derivatives on stock market volatility in India using the S and P CNX Nifty Index as a benchmark. They found clustering and persistence of volatility before and after derivatives, while listing seems to have no stabilization or destabilization effects on market volatility. The post-derivatives period showed that the sensitivity of the index returns to market returns and any day-of-the-week effects have disappeared. That is, the nature of the volatility patterns has altered during the post-derivatives period.

Nam, Yuhn, and Kim (2008)[54] investigated how the Asian financial crisis changed emerging markets in Asia by focusing on volatility spillovers and found that the influence of U.S. innovations on stock prices in Asia increased after the crisis.

Gregory James (2009)[55], examined the relationship between financial liberalisation and stock market volatility in Indonesia from April 11, 1983 to January 23, 2006. He found that capital market reforms coincided with a dramatic increase in stock market volatility but volatility significantly decreased when the market was opened to foreign investors. There was a significant rise in the volatility during the crisis. Volatility subsequently decreased two years and six years after the crisis and returned to the same level that had prevailed from the opening of the market.

Ruchika GAHLOT (2010)[56] examined the impact of derivative trading on stock market volatility. The sample data consist of closing prices of S and P CNX Nifty as well as closing prices of five derivative stocks and five non derivative stocks from April 1, 2002 to March 31, 2005. The study used GARCH model to capture nature of volatility over time and volatility clustering phenomenon of data. The evidences suggested that there was no significant change in the volatility of S and P CNX Nifty, but the structure of volatility has changed to some extent. However, results showed mixed effect in case of 10 individual stocks. These results can assist investors in making investment decision. It also helps to identify need for regulation.

Mantri and Gahan, (2012)[57] studied the volatility pattern of BSE sensitive index (Sensex) and NSE nifty (nifty) during the post derivative period. For this, it used models such as MA (Q,P), GARCH (Q, P), EGARCH (Q, P) AND IGARCH (Q, P) have been employed for the calculation of volatility in Sensex and nifty during pre-derivative period, post-derivative period and whole period of study. The impact of financial derivatives on the volatility of BSE Sensex and NSE nifty was significant under all the models. It is due to the derivatives, the daily volatility during post derivative period is low in comparison to pre-derivative and whole period.

2.4 Studies Related to Stock Market Integration

As stock markets world-wide have become more open there has been increasing interest in international linkages. Voluminous literature is available on stock market integration.

Kwan Sim, Cotsomitis (1995)[58] studied the stock markets of Australia, Japan, Hong Kong, Singapore, South Korea, Taiwan, the U.K, the U.S and Germany by employing monthly data from January, 1982 to February, 1991. Their evidence suggested that these markets were not weak form efficient as they found significant lead-lag relationships among equity markets.

Kim and Rogers (1995)[59] examined the repercussions on the relationship between the stock markets of Korea, Japan and United States after the Korean stock market liberalization announced in 1992. GARCH models are estimated to quantify the importance of volatility spillovers from Japan and US on the mean and variance of Korean returns. They evidenced that volatility Spillover has increased since the market liberalisationn.

Mohammad Najand (1996)[60] examined the direction of the causal relationship among the Asian stock markets namely Hong Kong, Singapore and Japan using state space modeling. They employed six years of daily stock returns from January 1984 to December, 1989. He concluded that Japan's stock market played an important role among the Asian stock markets during and after the crash of October, 1987 and the interactions among the Asian stock markets increased substantially after the crash.

Kam C. Chan, Benton E. Gup and Ming-Shiun Pan (1997)[61] analysed the international stock market efficiency and integration of eighteen countries namely Australia, Belgium, Canada, Denmark, Finland, France, Germany, India, Italy, Japan, Netherlands, Norway, Pakistan, Spain, Sweden, Switzerland, the United Kingdom and the United States covering a 32 year period from January, 1961 to December, 1992, with 384 monthly observations of each of the stock indices. Data were divided into four sub-samples (1960s, 1970s, the pre-October 1987 crash and the post-October 1987 crash. These markets were analysed both individually and collectively in regions to test for the weak form efficiency. They applied unit root test (ADF) and Johansen multivariate cointegration test. The empirical results evidenced that there was no significant cointegration for the full sample, the 1960s, the 1970s and after 1988. In the 1980s, before the stock market crash in 1987, there was significant cointegration and concluded that international diversification among the stock markets might be effective because the stock markets did not have long-run co-movements.

Kate Phylakktis and Fabiola Ravazzolo(1998)[62] investigated the stock market interactions among the group of Pacific-Basin stock markets (Hong-Kong, South Korea, Malaysia, Singapore, Taiwan and Thailand) and the industrialised countries of the Us and Japan. They had examined these issues by applying multivariate cointegration model in both the autoregressive and the moving average forms, over the period from1980 to 1998. They divided the sample period into two sub-periods, the pre liberalisation period ending in December 1989 and the post liberalisation sub-period covering the period between January 1990 and December 1998. According to them all the stock markets under investigation were not linked together in eighties and nineties and the international investors had opportunities for portfolio diversification by investing in most of the Pacific Basin countries.

Roca (1999)[63] investigated the price linkages between the equity markets of Australia and those of the U.S., the U.K., Japan, Hong Kong, Singapore, Taiwan and Korea using weekly stock market and found that no cointegration between Australia and other markets. But he found that the Granger causality tests revealed that Australia was significantly linked with the U.S and the U.K.

Asim Gosh (1999)[64] examined the Asian-Pacific stock markets by utilising the theory of cointegration to investigate, which developing markets are moved by the markets of Japan and the U.S. The data used in this study consisted of the daily closing values of the stock market index of the major exchange in each country. The sample indices were Hang Seng (HK), India BSE National (I), Korea SE Composite (K), Taiwan SE weighted (T), Kuala Lumpur Composite (M), Singapore All Share (S), S and P 500 Composite (US), and the NIKKEI 225 stock Average (JP) all expressed in terms of local currency. The period of study was from 26th March 1997 to 31st December 1997. It was found that the stock markets of Hong Kong, India, Korea and Malaysia were linked with the stock markets of the U.S. The stock markets of Indonesia, Philippines and Singapore were linked with the stock markets of Japan. The stock markets of Taiwan and Thailand did not appear to be influenced by the stock markets of the US or Japan.

Golaka C. Nath (2002)[65] carried out a study to understand how the level of financial liberalisation had helped Indian stock markets and other international equity markets. Two developed markets like NASDAQ and Japan and four emerging markets namely China, Singapore, Taiwan and India were chosen. The period from January, 1990 to November, 2002 was considered for the analysis except in case of NSE, data had been taken from July, 1990. The entire data were divided into ten-time span. Daily returns were used. The study results revealed that the Indian markets provided the best return with comparable risk as measured in terms of standard deviation for the entire period. The study did not find very significant correlation of S and P CNX Nifty with major markets. The same analysis was carried out on BSE SENSEX and S and P CNX Nifty for the period from January, 1995 to October, 2002. They established the fact that S and P CNX Nifty had lower volatility with higher return in comparison to BSE Sensex.

Jian Yang (2002)[66], examined long-run relationships and short-run dynamic causal linkages among the U.S., Japanese, and ten Asian emerging stock markets, with the particular attention to the 1997-1998 Asian financial crisis. Extending related empirical studies, comparative analyses of pre-crisis, crisis, and post-crisis periods are conducted to comprehensively evaluate how stock market integration was affected by financial crises. In general, the results for the case of Asia showed that both long-run co integration relationships and short run causal linkages among these markets were strengthened during the crisis and that these markets have generally been more integrated after the crisis than before the crisis.

Naeem Muhammad (2002)[67] examined whether the South Asian stock markets were interlinked and whether there was a link between South Asian stock markets and that of the stock market of the U.S. or U.K. The interdependence/dependence were examined for two periods: a period from January 1994 – December 1999 and from January 1994 – April 1998 (*i.e.*, pre-nuclear test period). For the entire sample, the results showed no cointegration among the South Asian markets and none of the South Asian market was cointegrated with either the U.S. or the U.K. market. However, the results of the pre-nuclear test period indicated that South Asian markets were cointegrated

Ali F. Darrat and Omar M. Benkato (2003)[68] investigated relations between the Istanbul Stock Exchange (ISE) and the major matured markets of the United States, Japan, and Europe. The data covered more than 14 years, spanning from January, 1986 to March, 2000 for a total of 171 monthly observations. They used ADF test, Phillips–Perron test and weighted symmetric to test the stationarity. Johansen Juselius (1990) efficient approach was used to test for cointegration among the five markets. GARCH (1, 1) model was used to know the volatility relations. Several conclusions emerged from the empirical analysis. First, there was a significant cointegration between ISE and the four matured markets. Second, Turkish market significantly integrated with the global market particularly in the post liberalisation period. Third the volatility in the ISE significantly linked with volatilities in the four matured markets only after the lifting of capital controls.

Tatsuyoshi Miyakoshi (2003)[69], examined the magnitude of return and volatility spillovers from Japan and the US to seven Asian equity markets. He concluded that only the influence of the US was important for Asian market returns; there was no influence from Japan. Secondly, the volatility of the Asian market was influenced more by the Japanese market than that of by the US. Thirdly, there existed an adverse influence of volatility from the Asian market to the Japanese market.

Click R., and Plummer M.G. (2003)[70] examined whether the ASEAN-5 markets were integrated or segmented using the time series technique of cointegration to extract a long-run relation. The empirical results suggested that the ASEAN-5 stock markets were cointegrated and were thus not completely segmented by national borders. They concluded that ASEAN-5 stock markets were integrated in the economic sense, but that integration was not complete. From the perspective of the international portfolio investor, benefits of international portfolio diversification across the five markets were reduced but not eliminated.

Asjeet Lamba (2004)[71] focused on the dynamic relationships between major developed markets and markets in India, Pakistan and Sri Lanka from July 1997 to February 2003. For India the S and P CNX Nifty was chosen. The major developed equity markets included in the analysis were France Germany, Japan, the UK and the US. He used multivariate cointegration and vector error correction modeling and arrived at the conclusion that Indian market was influenced by the large developed equity markets including the US, the UK, and Japan and that this influence was strengthened during the period from January, 2000 to February 2003. Pakistan and Sri Lanka markets were relatively isolated from the major developed markets during the entire sample period.

Harris and Pisedtasalasai (2005)[72] investigated return and volatility spillover effects between large and small stocks in the UK stock market using the multivariate AR-GJR GARCH-M model and found that the returns and volatilities of large stocks were important in predicting the future dynamics of smaller stocks, but that the returns and volatilities of smaller stocks had much less impact on the future dynamics of large stocks.

Hsiao, Cheng *et al.* (2005)[73], examined the long-run price relationship and the dynamic price transmission among the U.S., Germany, and four major Eastern European emerging stock markets, with particular attention to the impact of the 1998 Russian financial crisis. The results showed that both the long-run price relationship and the dynamic price transmission were strengthened among these markets after the crisis. After the crisis Germany influenced all the Eastern European markets but not before the crisis.

Wing-Keung, Aman Agarwal and Jun Du (2005)[74], empirically investigated the long-run equilibrium relationship and short-run dynamic linkage between the Indian stock market and the stock markets in major developed countries (United States, United Kingdom and Japan) after 1990 by examining the Granger causality relationship and the pairwise, multiple and fractional co integrations between the Indian stock market and the stock markets from these three developed markets covering the period from January 1, 1991 to December 31, 2003. They concluded that Indian stock market was integrated with mature markets and sensitive to the dynamics in these markets in a long run. In a short run, both US and Japan Granger cause the Indian stock market but not vice versa.

Yochanan Shachmurove (2005)[75] investigated the dynamic linkages across daily returns of stock market indexes in the Middle East countries (Egypt, Israel, Jordan, Lebanon, Morocco, Oman, and Turkey).and the United States and examined how a shock in one market was transmitted to other markets. The dynamic linkages among these stock markets were found to be relatively small. The conclusion was that although markets were efficient, there were dynamic linkages that could be explored and exploited to benefit the diversified international investors.

Kuper and Lestano (2006)[76] examined inter-financial market linkages and cross-border linkages in the emerging markets of Indonesia and Thailand, using daily data on short-term interest rates (which capture monetary policy), exchange rates and stock market returns for the period from March 3, 1995 to December 31, 2001. The outcomes indicated that the relationship among financial markets changed over the time and intensified during the Asian financial crisis. Evidence suggested that the linkages between financial markets were significantly affected by the crisis event

Hasem Ali Marashadeh (2006)[77] examined stock market integration in MENA represented by Turkey, Egypt, Jordon and Morocco and examined the integration between these markets and the developed markets represented by US, UK and Germany. The study covered the period from December 1994 to June 2004. The study indicated the presence of integration among the MENA markets especially when Egypt was dependent variable. No integration between MENA and other developed markets had been found except Egypt. Whereas the Granger causality test indicated that developed markets caused MENA stock markets and also all the MENA stock markets caused each other.

Valadkhani., A and Surachai Chancharat, (2007)[78] investigated the existence of cointegration and causality between the stock market price indices of Thailand and its major trading partners (Australia, Hong Kong, Indonesia, Japan, Korea, Malaysia, the Philippines, Singapore, Taiwan, the UK and the US), using monthly data spanning from December 1987 to December 2005. Both the Engle- Granger cointegration test and the Gregory and Hansen (1996) test (allowing for one structural break) provided no evidence of a long-run relationship between the stock prices of Thailand and these countries. However, in the short-run the scope of these opportunities was rather limited due to systematic and transitory fluctuations which are inherent to stock markets as evidenced by the causality test results

Dimitris Kenourgious *et al.* (2007)[79] have attempted to capture non-linear relationships in four emerging stock markets, namely Brazil, Russia, India, China (BRIC) and two developed markets (U.S. and U.K.), during the five recent financial crises (the Asian crisis, the Russian crisis, the tech bust and the two episodes in Brazil).Results provided evidence that there was an asymmetric increase in dependence among stock markets during all five crises. The jump in correlations and volatilities between stable and crisis periods supported financial contagion when crises were spread to other markets. Moreover, the differences in the magnitudes of the dependence changes showed that the industry-specific tech bust had a larger impact than country-specific crises. Furthermore, increases in tail dependence implied that the probability of markets crashing together was higher during periods of financial turmoil. A further finding of this study was that the multivariate regime-switching copula model captured higher level of dependence than the AG-DCC approach, possibly due to econometric reasons.

Hong Rim and Robert Setaputra (2008)[80] examined the process and trend of financial integration in Asia for a period from January 1992 to September 2006 and identified that financial markets in this region had not become more integrated during this period; the US influenced Asian financial markets; financial integration was not accompanied by financial efficiency; and financial integration reduced the negative effects of idiosyncratic shocks through cross-border portfolio diversification and capital mobility.

Siew-yen *et al.* (2008)[81] explored the co-movements between the stock indices of Singapore and five Asian Pacific economies and evidenced that the interdependence between these markets had intensified after the financial crisis. Before the crisis, only Malaysian stock market was found to be co integrated with Singapore but after the crisis Hong-Kong, Malaysia, Japan and US were found to be co integrated with the Singapore stock market. The stock market of Singapore was Granger – caused by that of Malaysia, but the causal relationship had weakened after the crisis.

Harju and Hussain (2008)[82] explored the dynamic first and second moment linkages among international equity markets using 5-minute index returns from the equity markets of the UK, Germany and the US, for the period from September, 2001 to August, 2003. The two European markets exhibited significant reciprocal return and volatility spillovers. This relationship appeared virtually unchanged by the presence or absence of the US market.

Bhar and Nikolova (2009)[83], examined the level of integration and the dynamic relationship between the BRIC countries, and found that India showed the highest level of regional and global integration among the BRIC countries, followed by Brazil and Russia and lastly by China. There was a negative relationship between the location conditional volatility of India with that of the Asia-Pacific region and of China with the world, which indicated a presence of diversification opportunities for portfolio investors and concluded that portfolio investors can continue to receive sound returns from taking positions in the index of these countries, however for an outstanding investment performance, they should consider investing in specific areas of growth within the economy rather than the country index.

Olowe, Rufus Ayodeji[84] investigated the relation between stock returns and volatility in Nigeria using E-GARCH-in-mean model in the light of banking reforms, insurance reform, stock market crash and the global financial crisis. Using daily returns over the period 4 January 2004 to January 9, 2009, Volatility persistence, asymmetric properties and risk return relationship were investigated for the Nigerian stock market. The result also showed that volatility was persistent and there was leverage effect supporting the work of Nelson (1991).The study found little evidence on the relationship between stock returns and risk as measured by its own volatility. The study found positive but insignificant relationship between stock return and risk. The result showed the banking reform in July 2004 and stock market crash since April 2008 negatively impacts on stock return while insurance reform and the global financial crisis have no impact on stock return. The stock market crash of 2008 is found to have contributed to the high volatility persistence in the Nigerian stock market especially during the global financial crisis period. The stock market crash was also found to have accounted for the sudden change in variance.

Janak Raj and Sarat Dhal1[85] investigated the nature of the financial integration of India's stock market with global and major regional markets. Empirical evidence supported the international integration of India's stock market in terms of stock prices measured in US dollars but not in local currency, a finding attributable to investment decisions of foreign investors. Correlations of daily stock price indices and returns suggested the integration of India's stock market with global and regional markets in the more recent period since 2003. There is evidence of the differential impact of regional and global stock markets on the Indian market in the long run as well as the short run. Within Asia, the Singapore and Hong Kong markets have significant influence, while the Japanese market has weak influence on the Indian market. The two global markets, the United States and the United Kingdom, could have a differential impact on the Indian market in the opposite direction, amid a structural shift in India's integration with these global markets. From a policy perspective, cointegrated stock markets would contribute to financial stability, since they cannot deviate too far from the long-run equilibrium path. From the standpoint of their portfolio diversification objective, investors cannot benefit from arbitrage activities in the long run. However, in the short run, markets would continue to be influenced by the portfolio diversification objective of foreign investors. The lack of evidence of integration of stock markets in terms of local currency gives rise to a concern that India's stock market integration may not be complete, a finding attributable to the inadequate role of domestic investors.

Anders C. Johansson (2009)[86] analyzed China's integration with major financial markets. Using conditional copulas, they showed that China has experienced an increasing level of integration with several major financial markets during the last decade, even though the countries financial markets are commonly seen as being insulated. Furthermore, the level of integration has increased with several major markets during the current financial crisis.

Saleem (2009)[87] examined the impact of Russia's 1998 financial crisis on the international linkage of the Russian market and suggested that after the crisis, the Russian market showed a bidirectional connection with the U.S. and Asian markets and a unidirectional relationship with emerging European markets.

Huyghebaert and Wang (2010)[88] examined the degree of stock markets integration among the seven major stock exchanges from developed and emerging countries such as; Hong Kong, Japan, Shanghai, Shenzhen, Singapore, South Korea and Taiwan. Their study also included the USA in the analysis to see the linkages with East Asian stock exchanges. Analysis conducted on pre-crisis, during-crisis and post-crisis (Asian financial crisis) by using daily data from July 1992 to June 2003. The Hong Kong and Singapore stock markets considerably responded to the shocks originating from other East Asian markets, particularly during financial crisis. During the post crisis period, shocks in Hong Kong and Singapore mainly influenced other East Asian markets (except mainland China). It was also observed that the associations between East Asian stock markets are time varying. The evidence showed that USA had significant influence on stock returns of East Asian markets (excluding mainland China) during all periods of study.

Komlavi Elubueni Assidenou (2011)[89] investigated the cointegration properties of major capital markets indices during the September, 2008 / August, 2009 episode of the financial and banking crises originated in U.S markets. Based on daily closing prices of international stock markets indices, the analysis showed that three set of indices of economies (OECD group, Pacific group and Asia group) have at least one cointegrating vector. Contrary to former studies that concluded on the independencies of Asian markets, this paper revealed that during the deeper financial crisis period, Asian major markets indices were cointegrated. This finding suggested that local investors in Asian capital markets cannot avoid any influence from outside capital markets even if some local markets were still entirely not opened to international investors.

Claus and Lucey (2012)[90] investigated the stock market integration between ten economies of Asia Pacific region. Results of this study indicate that the observed stock markets exhibit some degree of integration but the degree of segmentation varies among the ten economies. Further, it indicates that membership in a formal economic organization does not appear to influence the degree of integration.

To the best of our knowledge, this is the first study to examine the long-run relationship between Australia and several Asian markers considering the impact of crisis (Global Financial Crisis) by segmenting the data for before-crisis, during-crisis and after-crisis.

Even though there were many studies related to market efficiency, volatility and cointegration little attention was paid to emerging markets and the emerging markets were not compared with the developed markets. Hence, this study has been undertaken

References

1. Fama, F.E., "The Behaviour of Stock Market Prices", **Journal of Business,** Volume.38, No.1, January 1965, pp.34–105.
2. Grubel, H., "Internationally Diversified Portfolios: Welfare Gains and Capital Flows", **American Economic Reviews**, Vol.58, No.5, 1968, pp.1299–1314.
3. Conard, K. and Juttner, "Recent Behaviour of Stock Market Prices in Germany and the Random Walk Hypothesis", **Kyklos,** Vol.26, No.3, 1973, pp.576–599.
4. Bruno, H. Solnik, "Note on the Validity of the Random Walk for European Stock Prices", **The Journal of Finance,** Vol.28, No.5, 1973, pp.1151–1159.
5. Agmon, T., "The Relations among Equity Markets in the United States, United Kingdom, Germany and Japan", **The Journal of Finance**, Vol.26, No.4, 1972, pp.839–855.
6. James, C. Dyer, "Random Walks in Australian Share Prices: A Question of Efficient Capital Markets", **Australian Economic Papers**, Vol.12, December, 1976, pp.186–200.
7. Paul Barnes, "Thin Trading and Stock Market Efficiency: The Case of the Kuala Lumpur Stock Exchange", **Journal of Business Finance and Accounting**, Vol.13, No.4, 1986, pp.609–617.
8. Lo, A..W., and A.C. Mackinlay, "Stock Market Prices do not follow Random Walks: Evidence from a Simple Specification Test", **The Review of Financial Studies**, Vol.1, No.1, 1988 pp.41–66.
9. Skinner, D.J., "Options Markets and Stock Returns Volatility", **Journal of Financial Economics**, Vol.23, No.1, 1989, pp.61-78.

10. Taylor, M.P., and Tonks, I., "The Internationalisation of Stock Markets and Abolition of UK Exchange Control", **The Review of Economics and Statistics**, 1989, Vol.71, No.2, pp.332–336.
11. Rao, B.S.R., and Umesh Naik, "Inter – Relatedness of Stock Markets: Spectral investigation of U.S.A, Japanese and Indian Markets – Note", **Artha Vignana**, Vol. 32 No.3 and 4, 1990, pp.309–321.
12. Schwert, G.W., "Stock Market Volatility", **Financial Analysis Journal**, May –June 1990, pp.23-34.
13. Larry, J. Lockwood and Scott C. Linn, "An Examination of Stock Market Return Volatility During Overnight and Intraday Periods, 1964 -1989", **The Journal of Finance**, Vol.45, No.2, 1990, pp.591–601.
14. Theodore E. Day and Craig M. Lewis, "Stock Market Volatility and the Information Content of Stock Index Options", **Journal of Econometrics**, 1992, Vol.52, pp.267–287.
15. Kam, C. Chan, Benton E. Gup and Ming-Shiun Pan, "A Empirical Analysis of Stock Prices in Major Asian Markets and the United States", **The Financial Review**, Vol.27, No. 2, 1992, pp.289–307.
16. Kasa, K., "Common Stochastic Trends in International Stock Markets", **Journal of Monetary Economics**, Vol.29, No.1, 1992, p 95–124.
17. Richard Roll, "Industrial Structure and the Comparative behaviour of International Stock Market Indices", **The Journal of Finance**, Vol.47, No.1, 1992, pp.3–41.
18. John, P. Dickinson and Kinandu Muragu, "Market Efficiency in Developing Countries: A case Study of the Nairobi Stock Exchange", **Journal of Business Finance and Accounting**, Vol.21, No.1, 1994, pp.133–150.
19. Ramasastri, A.S., "Market Efficiency in the Nineties: Testing through Unit Root", **Prajnan,** Vol. 28, No.2, 1999–2000, pp.155–162.
20. Asma Mobarek Kevin Keasey, "Weak-Form Efficiency of an Emerging Market: Evidence from the Dhaka Stock Exchange of Bangladesh", The paper presented at the ENBS Conference held on OSLO May 2000. www.bath.ac.uk/cds/enbs-papers-pdfs/mobarek-new.pdf
21. Hyun-Jung Ryoo, Graham Smith, "Korean Stock Prices under Price Limits:VarianceRatioTestsofRandomWalks". www.Soas.ac.uk/department/departmentinfo.cfm?navid=469. 2000.
22. Sarath, P. Abeysekera, "Efficient Markets Hypothesis and the Emerging Capital Market in Sri Lanka: Evidence from the Colombo Stock Exchange – A Note", **Journal of Business Finance and Accounting**, vol.28, No.1 and 2, 2001, pp.249–261.
23. Ramasastri, A.S., "Concept of Relative Efficiency Application to Indian Stock Markets in the 1990s", **Prajnan,** Vol.30, No.2, 2001, pp.199–212.

24. Pradhan, H.K and Lakshmi S. Narasimhan, "Stock Price Behaviour in India since Liberalization", **Asia-Pacific Development Journal**, Vol.9, No.2, 2002, pp.84–107.

25. Chandra Babu and Punithavathy Pandian, "Efficiency of Indian Stock Indices", **NSE News**, June 2002, pp.11–14, and 18.

26. Sunil Poshakwale, "The Random Walk Hypothesis in the Emerging Indian Stock Market", **Journal of Business Finance and Accounting**, Vol.29, No.9 and 10, 2002, pp.1275–1299.

27. Chaudhuri, K. and Wu, Y., 2003, "Random walk versus breaking trend in stock prices: Evidence from emerging markets," **Journal of Banking and Finance**, Vol. 27(4), pages 575-592

28. Hasan, M. S., 2004, "On the Validity of the Random Walk Hypothesis Applied to the Dhaka Stock Exchange," **International Journal of Theoretical and Applied Finance**, Vol. 7, Issue 8; p. 106

29. Oktay Tas and Salim Dursunoglu, "Testing Random Walk Hypothesis for Istanbul Stock Exchange", Paper presented at 15th International conference of International Trade and Finance Association year May 2005 Paper 38. http://services.bepress.com/itfa/15 th/art38.

30. Natalia Abrosimova and Gishan Dissanaike : "Testing the Weak-Form Efficiency of the Russian Stock Market", April 2005.

31. Lean, H.H. and R. Smyth, 2007, "Do Asian Stock Markets Follow a Random Walk? Evidence from LM Unit Root Tests with One and Two Structural Breaks," **Review of Pacific Basin Financial Markets and Policies.** Vol. 10, Issue. 1; pg. 15

32. Rakesh Gupta and Parikshit K. Basu : "Weak Form Efficiency In Indian Stock Markets" **International Business and Economics Research Journal** – March 2007 Volume 6, Number 3 57

33. Purna Chandra Padhan:"The Random Walk Hypothesis Pertaining to Stock Prices in India: A Firm Level Analysis" **MIBES Transactions**, Vol 3, Issue 1, Spring 2009 63-78

34. Ibrahim Awad and Zahran Daraghma "Testing the Weak-Form Efficiency of the Palestinian Securities Market" **International Research Journal of Finance and Economics** ISSN 1450-2887 Issue 32 (2009)

35. Daniel Weaver, "Intraday Volatility on the NYSE and NASDAQ", www. http//:nyse.com /market info/researchpaper/1050241176674/.html_7k. 2000.

36. Thenmozhi, M.,"Futures Trading Information and Spot Price Volatility of NSE 50 Index Future Contract, **NSE News**, September, 2002, pp.8–11.

37. Samanta, G.P., "Stock Market Return, Volatility and Future Output Growth – Some Observations Relating to Indian Economy", **NSE News**, August 2003, pp.3-6.

38. Golaka, C. Nath, "Behaviour of Stock Market Volatility after Derivatives", **NSE News**, November, 2003, pp.3–13.

39. George, C. Pardee and Helennn C. Pardee, "Stock Market Volatility and Monetary Policy: What the Historical Records Shows", **Working paper prepared for the Reserve Bank of Australia's annual research conference,** Sydney. August 2003. www.rba.gov.publications and research/conferences /2003/Eichengreen_Tong.pdf.

40. Charles, P. Johnson et. al., "Analysing Stock Market Volatility Using Extreme Day Measures", **The Journal of Financial Research**, Vol.27, No.4, 2004, pp.585–601.

41. Golaka, C. Nath, "Integration of Global Equity Markets – A case for India", **NSE News**, November 2002, pp.11–16.

42. Julan Du and Shang-Jin Wei, "Does Insider Trading Raise Market Volatility", **The Economic Journal**, Vol.114, No.498, 2004, pp.916–942.

43. Parthapratim Pal, "Recent Volatility in Stock Markets in India and Foreign Institutional Investors", www.networkideas.org/featart/nov2004/fa24_ volatility _stock_market.htm.

44. Lieven Baele "Volatility Spillover Effects in European Equity Markets"

45. Madhusudanan Karmakar, "Modeling Conditional Volatility of the Indian Stock Markets, **Vikalpa,** Vol.30, No.3, 2005, pp.21–37.

46. Golaka, C.,Nath and Manoj Dalvi, "A Suitable Volatility Measure in Indian Stock Market", **The ICFAI Journal of Applied Finance**, October, 2005, pp.16–22.

47. Ajey Pandey, "Volatility Models and their Performance in Indian Capital Markets", **Vikalpa,** Vol. 30. No.2, 2005, pp.27–46.

48. Siong Hook Law: "Has Stock Market Volatility in the Kuala Lumpur Stock Exchange Returned to Pre-Asian Financial Crisis Levels?" **ASEAN Economic Bulletin** Vol. 23, No. 2 (2006), pp. 212-29

49. Frimpong Joseph and Oteng-Abayie: "Modelling and Forecasting Volatility of Returns on the Ghana Stock Exchange Using Garch Models", **American Journal of Applied Sciences** 3 (10): 2042-2048, 2006.

50. Rajni Mala and Mahendra Reddy "Measuring Stock Market Volatility in an Emerging Economy" **International Research Journal of Finance and Economics**

51. Cuñado. J, Gil-Alana and Perez de Gracia "Stock Market Volatility in US Bull and Bear Markets" Journal of Money, **Investment and Banking** Issue 1 (2008) *www.eurojournals.com/jmib1 per cent 20cunado.pdf*

52. Lucía de las Nieves Morales (2008), "Volatility Spillovers between Equity and Currency Markets: Evidence from Major Latin American Countries" **Cuadernos de eConomí a,** Vol. 45 (noViembre), pp. 185-215, 2008

53. Mallikarjunappa1 T. and Afsal E. M "The Impact of Derivatives on Stock Market Volatility: A Study of the Nifty Index" **Asian Academy of Management Journal of Accounting and Finance**

54. Nam, Joo Ha, Yuhn, Ky-hyang and Kim, Sang Bong. "What Happened to Pacific-basin Emerging Markets after the 1997 Financial Crisis?" **Applied Financial Economics,** Vol. 18, No. 8, pp. 639-658.

55. Gregory James : "Financial Liberalisation and Stock Market Volatility: The Case of Indonesia" www.papers.ssrn.com/sol3/papers.cfm?abstract_id=302851

56. Ruchika GAHLOT, Saroj K. DATTA and Sheeba KAPIL "Impact of Derivative Trading On Stock Market Volatility in India: A Study of S and P CNX Nifty" **Eurasian Journal of Business and Economics** 2010, 3 (6), 139-149

57. Mantri, J., and Gahan, P. "Volatitlity study of indian stock market during its post derivative" period.

58. Kwan, A. A. Sim and J. Cotsomitis, "The Causal Relationships between Equity Indices on World Exchanges", **Applied Economics**, Vol.27, No.1, 1995, pp.33–37.

59. Kim and Rogers (2005), "International Stock Price Spillovers and Market Liberalisation: Evidence from Japan, Korea and the United States" http://www.federalreserve.gov/pubs/ifdp/1995/499/ifdp499.pdf (application/pdf)

60. Mohammad Najand, "A Causality Test of the October Crash of 1987: Evidence from Asian Stock Markets", **Journal of Business Finance and Accounting**, Vol.23, No.3, 1996, pp.439–448.

61. Kam, C. Chan, Benton E. Gup and Ming-Shiun Pan, "International Stock Market Efficiency and Integration: A Study of Eighteen Nations", **Journal of Business Finance and Accounting**, Vol.24, No.6, 1997, pp.803–813.

62. Kate Phylakktis and Fabiola Ravazzolo, "Stock Market in Emerging Markets:Implications for International Portfolio Diversification". http:// www.papers.ssrn.com/sol3/papers.cfm?= 562922.

63. Roca, E.D., "Short-term and Long –term Price Linkages between the equity Markets of Australia and Its Major Trading Partners", **Applied Financial Economics**, Vol.9, No.5, 1999, pp.501–511.

64. Asim Ghosh Reza Saidi and Keith H. Johnson, "Who Moves the Asia – Pacific Stock Markets – US or Japan? Empirical Evidence Based on the Theory of Cointegration", **The Financial Review,** Vol. 34, No.1, 1999, pp.159–170.

65. Golaka, C. Nath and Sunil Verma, "Study of Common Trend and Integration in the Emerging Stock – A Case Study of India, Singapore and Taiwan", **NSE News**, July 2003, pp.6- 12.

66. Jian Yang *et al.*, "Stock market integration and financial crises: the case of Asia" **Applied Financial Economics** (forthcoming)

67. Ali, F. Darrat and Omar M. Benkato, "Interdependence and Volatility Spillovers Under Market Liberalisation: The Case of Istanbul Stock Exchange", **Journal of Business Finance and Accounting**, Vol.30, No.7 and 8, 2003, pp.1089–1114.

68. Tatsuyoshi Miyakoshi (2003), "Spillovers of stock return volatility to Asian equity markets from Japan and the US", **Journal of Financial Markets, Institutions and Money**. Volume 13, Issue 4, October 2003, Pages 383-399 http://www.sciencedirect.com/science/journal/10424431

69. Click, R. W. and Plummer, M.G. (2005), "Stock Market Integration in ASEAN After the Asian Financial Crisis", **Journal of Asian Economics**, 16 (1), 5-28.

70. Asjeet, S. Lamba, "Who Moves Equity Markets in the Indian Subcontinent?", **NSE News**, February 2004, pp.3–7.

71. Harris D. F. Richard and Anirut Pisedtasalasai, (2005), "Return and Volatility Spillovers Between Large and Small Stocks in the UK", Xfi Centre for Finance and Investment University of Exeter, **UK Paper Number: 06/09.**

72. Jian Yang, Cheng Hsiao (2005), "The Emerging Market Crisis and Stock Market Linkages:Further Evidence" **IEPR WORKING PAPER** 05.27, http://www.usc.edu/iepr

73. Wing-Keung Aman Agarwal and Jun Du (2005) Financial Integration for India Stock Market, a Fractional Cointegration Approach http://nt2.fas.nus.edu.sg/ecs/pub/wp/wp0501.pdf

74. Yochanan Shachmurove (2005) Dynamic Linkages Among the Emerging Middle Eastern and the United States Stock Markets **International Journal of Business**, 10(1), 2005, 104-132.

75. Kuper.H and Lestano (2006) "Dynamic conditional correlation analysis of financial market interdependence: An application to Thailand and Indonesia" CCSO Working paper 2006/02, http://www.eco.rug.nl/ccso. Hsiao, Cheng *et al.* (2005), "The Emerging Market Crisis and Stock Market Linkages Further Evidence" **papers.ssrn.com/sol3/papers.cfm?abstract_id=782424**

76. Hasem Ali Marashadeh : (2006) "Financial Integration of the MENA emerging stock Markets. **Thesis**.

77. Valadkhani, A., Chancharat†Dynamic, S. (2008), "Dynamic Linkages Between Thai and International Stock Markets", **Journal of Economic Studies**, 2008, http://ro.uow.edu.au/commpapers/354

78. Dimitris Kenourgious *et al.* (2007) Financial Crises and Contagion: Evidence for BRIC Stock Markets **http://papers.ssrn.com/sol3/cf_dev/AbsByAuth.cfm?per_id=406881**

79. Hong Rim, and Robert Setaputra, (2008), "Studies On The Financial Integration And Market Efficiency: Empirical Evidence From Asia" **IABR and TLC Conference Proceedings San Juan, Puerto Rico, USA**

80. Siew-Yen F, Wing Keung Wong and Terence Tai-Leung Chong (2008), "Are the Asian Equity Markets More Interdependent After the Financial Crisis?", **Economics Bulletin,** Vol. 6, No. 16, pp. 1-7.

81. Harju K. and Hussain S.M. (2008), "Intraday Return and Volatility Spillovers Across International Equity Markets", **International Research Journal of Finance and Economics**, Issue 22.

82. Bhar R and Nikolova B (2009), "Return, Volatility Spillovers and Dynamic Correlation in the BRIC Equity Markets: An Analysis Using a Bivariate EGARCH Framework", **Global Finance Journal**, Vol. 9, No. 3, pp. 203-218.

83. Olowe, Rufus Ayodeji (2009) "Stock Return, Volatility And The Global Financial Crisis In An Emerging Market: The Nigerian Case" **International Review of Business Research Papers** Vol. 5 No. 4 June 2009 Pp. 426-447

84. Janak Raj and Sarat Dhal "Integration of India's Stock Market with Global and Major Regional Markets" **BIS Papers No 42**

85. Anders C Johansson (2010) "China's Financial Market Integration with the World," **Journal of Chinese Economic and Business Studies** Volume 8, Issue 3, 293-314

86. Saleem, Kashif. 2009. "International Linkage of the Russian Market and the Russian Financial Crisis: A Multivariate GARCH Analysis." **Research in International Business and Finance**, Vol. 23, No. 3, pp. 243-256.

87. Huyghebaert, N., and Wang, L. (2010) "The Co-movement of Stock Markets in East Asia Did the 1997-1998 Asian Financial Crisis Really Strengthen Stock Market Integration?" **China Economic Review**, 21, 98-112.

88. Komlavi Elubueni (2011) "Cointegration of Major Stock Market Indices during the 2008 Global Financial Distress" **International Journal of Economics and Finance** Vol. 3, No. 2; May 2011

89. Claus, E., and Lucey, B.M. (2012) "Equity Market Integration in the Asia Pacific Region: Evidence from Discount Factors" Research in International Business and Finance, 26, 137-163. **Eurasian Journal of Business and Economics** 2010, 3 (6), 139-149.

Chapter 3

Features and Characteristics of the International Stock Markets

3.1 Introduction

Market capitalization is a good indicator of the health of capital markets. Market capitalization means the total number of outstanding shares of the company multiplied by the share price of that stock. Stock market capitalization means the total market capitalization of all the individual stocks that are listed on the exchange. The size and growth of the market capitalisation is a critical measurement of a stock exchange's success or failure. The stock price movement determines the market capitalization. Market capitalization is calculated by multiplying a company's shares outstanding by the current market price of one share. The investment community uses this figure to determine a company's size, as opposed to sales or total asset figures. It reflects how much it would cost to purchase the entire company at the current share value. The market capitalization of companies is grouped together into small, mid and large-cap companies. It is a good yard stick to portfolio diversification.

3.2 An Overview of Stock Exchanges in Developing Countries

3.2.1 The Stock Exchange in India

India is among the top emerging markets in South Asia with almost more than 20 regional stock exchanges. The Bombay Stock Exchange and the National Stock Exchange of India Ltd. are the two primary exchanges in India. They are the two leading exchanges account for about 80 per cent of the equity volume traded in India.

The **National Stock Exchange of India Limited** (**NSE**) NSE was established in 1992 as the first demutualized electronic exchange in the country in Mumbai. NSE was the first exchange in the country to provide a modern, fully automated screen-based electronic trading system which offered easy trading facility to the investors spread across the length and breadth of the country.

NSE's flagship index, the CNX Nifty,the 50 stock index, is used extensively by investors in India and around the world as a barometer of the Indian capital markets. NSE has been established with domestic and global investors. NSE offers trading, clearing and settlement services in equity, equity derivatives, debt and currency derivatives segments. It is the first exchange in India to introduce electronic trading facility thus connecting together the investor base of the entire country.

NSE was also instrumental in creating the National Securities Depository Limited (NSDL) which allows investors to securely hold and transfer their shares and bonds electronically. The NSDL's security, combined with the transparency, lower transaction prices and efficiency that NSE offered, greatly increased the attractiveness of the Indian stock market to domestic and international investors.

NSE offers trading in the following segments:

Equities

- ✰ Equities
- ✰ Indices
- ✰ Mutual Funds
- ✰ Exchange Traded Funds
- ✰ Initial Public Offerings
- ✰ Security Lending and Borrowing Scheme

Derivatives

- ✰ Equity Derivatives (including Global Indices like CNX 500, Dow Jones and FTSE)
- ✰ Currency Derivatives
- ✰ Interest Rate Futures

Debt

- ✰ Corporate Bonds

Equity Derivatives

3.2.2 The Stock Exchange in Indonesia

Indonesia Stock Exchange is based in Jakarta, Indonesia. Originally established in 1912 under the Dutch colonial government, it was re-opened in 1977 after several closures during World War I and World War II. In Indonesia, market capitalisation was high in September 2007. In September 2007, Jakarta Stock Exchange and Surabaya Stock Exchange merged and named Indonesian Stock Exchange by Indonesian Minister of Finance. After the merger, the new entity has seven directors.

Managers setting strategies based on Singapore and Hong Kong stock exchange, as well as brokers from Central and Eastern Indonesia which makes up 5 per cent of the brokers all around the country.

Table 3.1: Market Capitalisation and GDP for India and Indonesia (2000–2012)
($ US in Millions/Billions)

Year	*India Market Capitalization $ USD Millions*	*India-GDP $ USD Billions*	*Indonesia Market Capitalization $ USD Millions*	*Indonesia-GDP $ USD Billions*
2000	148063	464.30	268342	140.00
2001	110395	474.70	230056	165.02
2002	131010	492.40	299913	160.45
2003	279092	522.80	546590	195.66
2004	387851	617.60	732506	234.77
2005	553074	721.60	814281	256.84
2006	818878	834.20	1388863	285.87
2007	1819100	949.10	2116929	364.57
2008	645477	1238.70	987605	432.22
2009	1179235	1224.10	1781909	510.23
2010	1615860	1365.40	3603880	539.58
2011	1015370	1708.50	3901068	755.10
2012	1263335	1835.81	3967721	892.97

In India market capitalization was very low in the year 2001 because of dot.com problem. The total market capitalisation was very high in the year 2007 (1,819,100 $US million). The total market capitalisation declined in the year 2001 due to

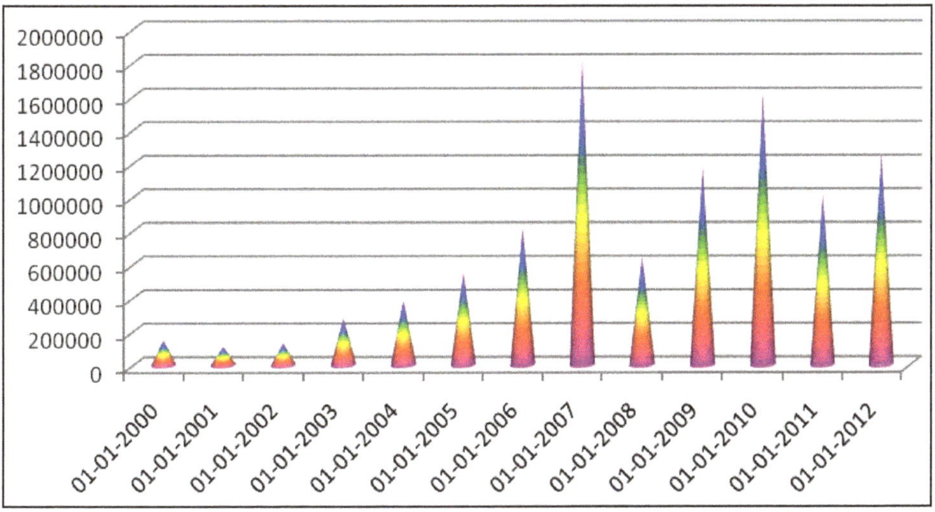

Figure 3.1: Market Capitalization in India Stock Exchange (2000–2012) $US Millions.

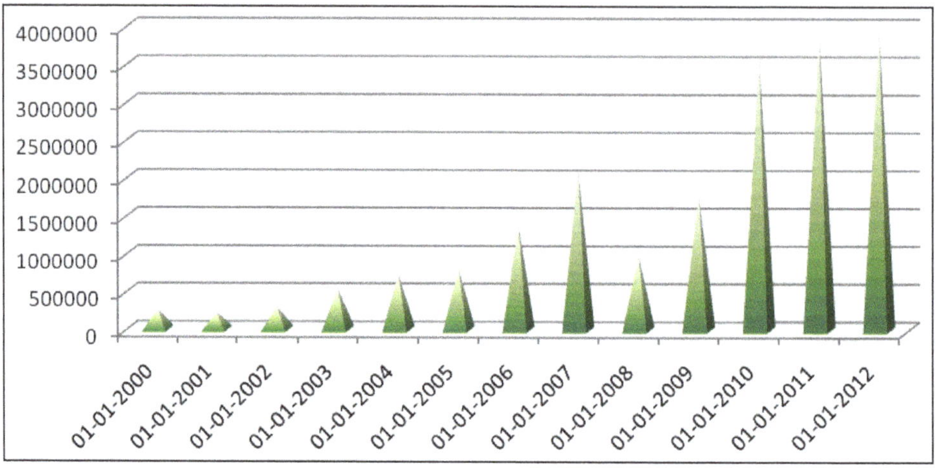

Figure 3.2: Market Capitalization in Indonesia Stock Exchange (2000–2012) $US Millions.

significant slowdown of the industrial sector and unsatisfactory performance of infrastructure industries and this set bear phase in the market. As on 31st March 2012 the total market capitalisation was $ US 12, 63, 335 Million. India is developing into an open-market economy, yet traces of its past autarkic policies remain. Economic liberalization measures, including industrial deregulation, privatization of state-owned enterprises, and reduced controls on foreign trade and investment, began in the early 1990s and served to accelerate the country's growth, which averaged under 7 per cent per year from 1997 to 2011.

India's diverse economy encompasses traditional village farming, modern agriculture, handicrafts, a wide range of modern industries, and a multitude of services. Slightly less than half of the work force is in agriculture, but, services are the major source of economic growth, accounting for nearly two-thirds of India's output with less than one-third of its labor force. India has capitalized on its large educated English-speaking population to become a major exporter of information technology services, business outsourcing services, and software workers. India's economic growth began slowing in 2011 because of a decline in investment caused by high interest rates, rising inflation, and investor pessimism about the government's commitment to further economic reforms and about the global situation. The outlook for India's long-term growth is moderately positive due to a young population and corresponding low dependency ratio, healthy savings and investment rates, and increasing integration into the global economy.

In Indonesia there was a steady growth in market capitalization from 2000–2007 but in 2008 its market capitalization was very low because of global financial crisis. Afterwards market experienced upward trend. Market capitalisation was very high in 20011 and 2012. At end of 2010, the capitalisation was US $ 3,603,880 miillion and 26 percent of it are 17 state-owned companies listed among 421 companies listed. In 3 June 2011 there are 344,279 local investors registered at the IDX Custodian (KSEI). As of the end of 2011, foreigners owned 60 percent of shares. As end of 2012, the Indonesia Stock Exchange had 462 listed companies with a combined market capitalisation of US $ 39,67,721 billion.

3.2.3 The Stock Exchange in Malaysia

The **Kuala Lumpur Stock Exchange** (KLSE, **Bursa Saham Kuala Lumpur** in Malay) dates back to 1930 when the Singapore Stockbrokers' Association was set up as a formal organisation dealing in securities in Malaya. By 1960, the Malayan Stock Exchange was formed and public trading of shares began on 9 May. The Stock Exchange of Malaysia was officially formed in 1964 and in the following year, with the secession of Singapore from Malaysia, the common stock exchange continued to function under the name Stock Exchange of Malaysia and Singapore (SEMS).

In 1973, with the termination of currency interchangeability between Malaysia and Singapore, the SEMS was separated into The Kuala Lumpur Stock Exchange Bhd (KLSEB) and The Stock Exchange of Singapore (SES). Malaysian companies continued to be listed on SES and vice versa. A new company limited by guarantee, The Kuala Lumpur Stock Exchange (KLSE) took over operations of KLSEB as the stock exchange. In 1994, it was renamed Kuala Lumpur Stock Exchange.

3.2.4 The Stock Exchange in Korea

Korea Exchange (**KRX**) is the sole securities exchange operator in South Korea. It is headquartered in Busan, and has an office for cash markets and market oversight in Seoul. The Korea Exchange was created through the integration of Korea Stock Exchange, Korea Futures Exchange and KOSDAQ Stock Market under the Korea Stock and Futures Exchange Act. The securities and derivatives markets of former exchanges are now business divisions of Korea Exchange: the Stock Market Division, KOSDAQ Market Division and Derivatives Market Division.

KOSPI offers trading in the following segments:

- ☆ Stocks
- ☆ Bonds
- ☆ Exchange Traded Funds (ETFs)
- ☆ Exchange-Linked Warrants (ELWs)
- ☆ Real Estate Investment Trusts (REITs)

The market capitalization and GDP for Malaysia and Korea markets are given in Table 3.2.

Bank Negara Malaysia (the central bank) maintains healthy foreign exchange reserves; a well-developed regulatory regime has limited Malaysia's exposure to riskier financial instruments and the global financial crisis. Malaysian stock market capitalization was steadily increasing from 2000 to 2007. In 2008 it tumbled down due to global financial crisis afterwards the market rebounded.

South Korea over the past four decades has demonstrated incredible economic growth and global integration to become a high-tech industrialized economy. In the 1960s, GDP per capita was comparable with levels in the poorer countries of Africa and Asia. In 2004, South Korea joined the trillion-dollar club of world economies.

Table 3.2: Market Capitalization and GDP of Malaysia and Korea (2000–2012) ($ US in Millions/Billions)

Year	*Malaysia Market Capitalization $ USD Millions*	*Malaysia -GDP $ USD Billions*	*Korea Market Capitalization $ USD Millions*	*Korea-GDP $ USD Billions*
2000	116934	79.65	171586	486.30
2001	120007	93.79	220045	561.63
2002	123872	92.78	249638	533.05
2003	168376	100.85	329615	609.02
2004	190010	110.20	428648	680.52
2005	181235	124.75	718180	764.88
2006	235355	143.53	835188	898.13
2007	325663	162.69	1123632	1011.80
2008	187065	193.55	494630	1122.60
2009	255952	230.81	836461	1002.22
2010	410534	202.26	1089216	901.93
2011	395082	247.53	994301	1094.50
2012	476340	287.33	1180473	1202.46

A system of close government and business ties, including directed credit and import restrictions, initially made this success possible. The government promoted the import of raw materials and technology at the expense of consumer goods, and encouraged savings and investment over consumption. South Korea adopted numerous economic reforms following the crisis, including greater openness to foreign investment and imports. Growth moderated to about 4 per cent annually

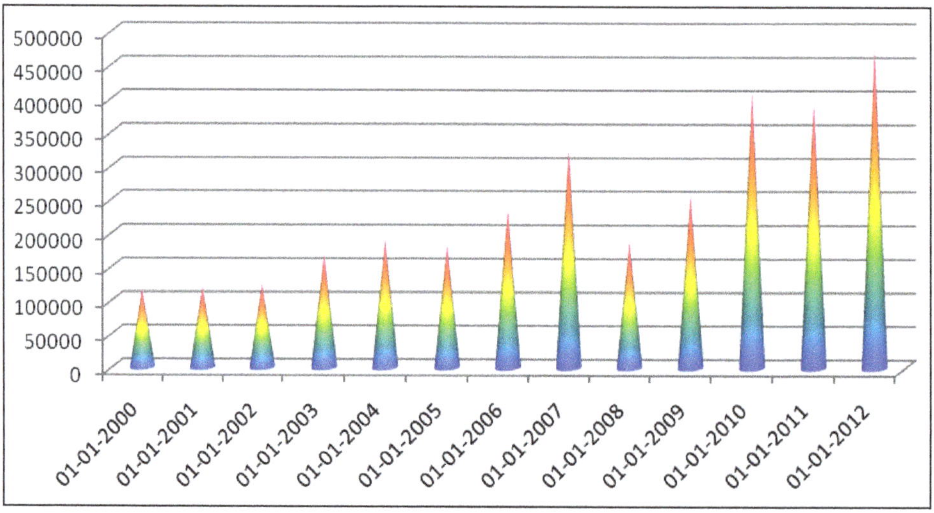

Figure 3.3: Market Capitalization in Malaysia Stock Exchange (2000–2012) $US Millions.

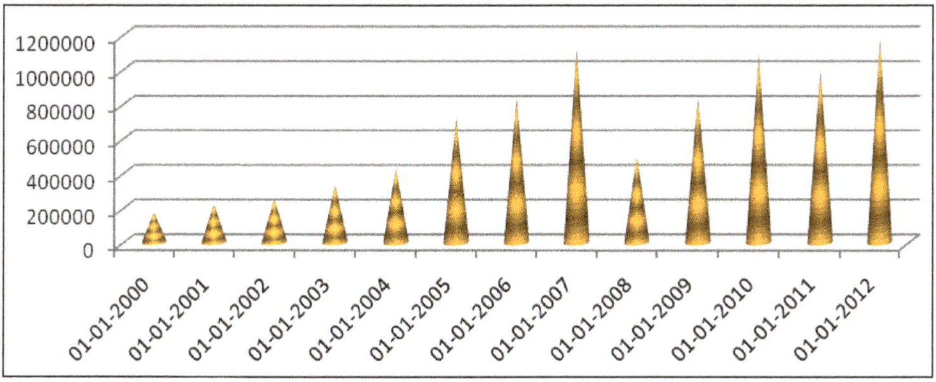

Figure 3.4: Market Capitalization in Korea Stock Exchange (2000–2012) $US Millions.

between 2003 and 2007. South Korea's export focused economy was hit hard by the 2008 global economic downturn, but quickly rebounded in subsequent years, reaching over 6 per cent growth in 2010. The US-Korea Free Trade Agreement was ratified by both governments in 2011 and went into effect in March 2012.

3.2.5 Stock Exchange in China

The **Shanghai Stock Exchange** is a stock exchange that is based in the city of Shanghai, China. Unlike the Hong Kong Stock Exchange, the Shanghai Stock Exchange is still not entirely open to foreign investors due to tight capital account controls exercised by the Chinese mainland authorities and often manipulated by the decisions of the Central Government.

The Shanghai Clearing House provides security for financial market participants, and efficient clearing services development purposes, but also conducive to international peers inter-agency communication and cooperation. It provides central counterparty clearing of foreign currency in the interbank market, including clearing, settlement, margin management, collateral management, information services, consulting services, and related management department under other business.

The securities listed at the SSE include the three main categories of stocks, bonds, and funds. Bonds traded on SSE include treasury bonds (T-bond), corporate bonds, and convertible corporate bonds. SSE T-bond market is the most active of its kind in China. There are two types of stocks being issued in the Shanghai Stock Exchange: "A" shares and "B" shares. A shares are priced in the local renminbi yuan currency, while B shares are quoted in U.S. dollars. Initially, trading in A shares are restricted to domestic investors only while B shares are available to both domestic (since 2001) and foreign investors.

3.2.6 Stock Exchange in Taiwan

The **Taiwan Stock Exchange Corporation** (**TWSE**) is a financial institution, located in Taipei, Taiwan. The TWSE was established in 1961 and began operating as a stock exchange on 9 February 1962. It is regulated by the Financial Supervisory Commission. As of 31 December 2012, the Taiwan Stock Exchange had 758 listed companies with a combined market capitalization of NT$24,519,622 million. The exchange has normal trading sessions from 09:30am to 05:30pm and post-market sessions from 05:30pm to 06:00pm on all days of the week except Saturdays, Sundays and holidays declared by the exchange in advance. The market capitalization and GDP for China and Taiwan markets are given in Table 3.3.

Table 3.3: Market Capitalization and GDP of China and Taiwan (2000–2012)

($ US.in Millions/Billions)

Year	*China Market Capitalization $ USD Millions*	*China-GDP $ USD Billions*	*Taiwan Market Capitalization $ USD Millions*	*Taiwan-GDP $ USD Billions*
2000	623397	1089.45	NA	299.01
2001	506072	1205.26	"	326.16
2002	463084	1332.24	"	293.69
2003	551236	1461.91	"	301.10
2004	665248	1649.92	"	310.54
2005	693486	1941.75	"	340.01
2006	895249	2268.59	"	364.85
2007	1162565	2729.78	"	376.33
2008	1328837	3523.09	"	393.11
2009	915825	4558.43	"	400.20
2010	1079640	5059.42	"	377.57
2011	889596	6039.42	"	428.22
2012	1108127	7492.43	"	465.20

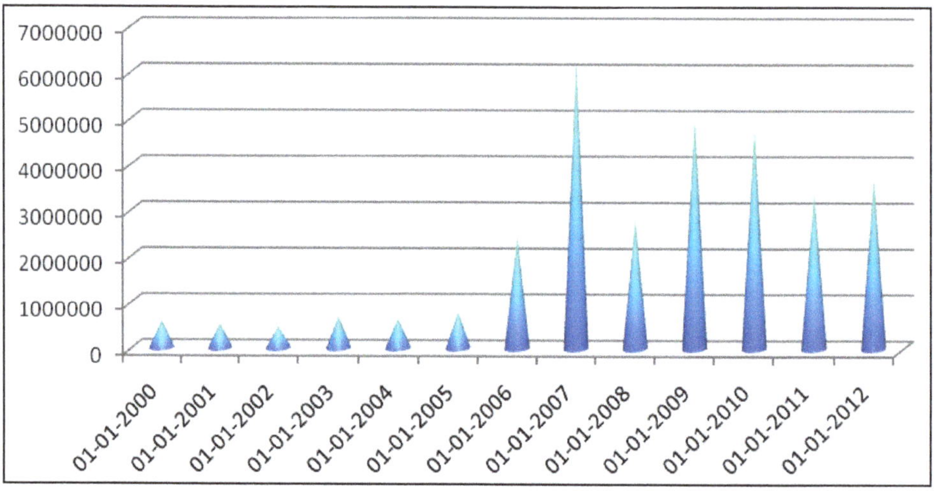

Figure 3.5: Market Capitalization in China Stock Exchange (2000–2012) $US Millions.

After keeping its currency tightly linked to the US dollar for years, in July 2005 China moved to an exchange rate system that references a basket of currencies. From mid 2005 to late 2008 cumulative appreciation of the renminbi against the US dollar was more than 20 per cent, but the exchange rate remained virtually pegged to the dollar from the onset of the global financial crisis until June 2010, when Beijing allowed resumption of a gradual appreciation.

2006 - The SSE resumed full operation as the yearlong ban on IPOs was lifted in May. The world's second largest (US$21.9 billion) IPO by the Industrial and Commercial Bank of China (ICBC) was launched in both Shanghai and Hong Kong stock markets

In 2010 China became the world's largest exporter. Reforms began with the phasing out of collectivized agriculture, and expanded to include the gradual liberalization of prices, fiscal decentralization, increased autonomy for state enterprises, growth of the private sector, development of stock markets and a modern banking system, and opening to foreign trade and investment. China has implemented reforms in a gradualist fashion. In recent years, China has renewed its support for state-owned enterprises in sectors considered important to "economic security," explicitly looking to foster globally competitive industries.

Several factors are converging to slow China's growth, including debt overhang from its credit-fueled stimulus program, industrial overcapacity, inefficient allocation of capital by state-owned banks, and the slow recovery of China's trading partners. The government's 12th Five-Year Plan, adopted in March 2011, emphasized continued economic reforms and the need to increase domestic consumption in order to make the economy less dependent in the future on fixed investments, exports, and heavy industry.

Taiwan has a dynamic capitalist economy with gradually decreasing government guidance of investment and foreign trade. Exports, led by electronics, machinery, and petrochemicals have provided the primary impetus for economic development. This heavy dependence on exports exposes the economy to fluctuations in world demand. Taiwan's diplomatic isolation, low birth rate, and rapidly aging population are other major long-term challenges. Taiwan's total fertility rate of just over one child per woman is among the lowest in the world, raising the prospect of future labor shortages, falling domestic demand, and declining tax revenues. Taiwan's population is aging quickly, with the number of people over 65 expected to account for nearly 20 per cent of the island's total population by 2025.

Closer economic links with the mainland bring greater opportunities for Taiwan's economy but also pose new challenges as the island becomes more economically dependent on China at a time when political differences remain unresolved. During 2014, the press paid increasing attention to domestic economic issues, while pushing aside the debates over trade liberalization that were a hallmark of MA's tenure. The media focused on the divide between Taiwan's "haves" and "have nots," providing extensive coverage of public frustration with stagnant wages, skyrocketing housing prices, and the difficulty of finding decent entry-level jobs.

3.3 An Overview of Stock Exchanges in Developed Countries

3.3.1 The Stock Exchange in Australia

The ASX (Australian Stock Exchange Limited) was formed in 1987 by legislation of the Australian Parliament which enabled the amalgamation of six independent stock exchanges that formerly operated in the state capital cities. After demutualisation, the ASX was the first exchange in the world to have its shares quoted on its own market. The ASX was listed on 14 October 1998. On 7 July 2006 the Australian Stock Exchange merged with SFE Corporation, holding company for the Sydney Futures Exchange.

Australia was ranked 5th out of 57 of the world's leading financial systems and capital markets by the World Economic Forum; The 8th largest in the world (based on free-float market capitalisation) and the 2nd largest in Asia-Pacific, with A$1.2 trillion market capitalisation and average daily secondary trading of over A$5 billion a day; 3rd largest debt market in the Asia Pacific; largest fixed income derivatives in the Asia-Pacific region; The Australian foreign exchange market is the 7th largest in the world in terms of global turnover, while the Australian dollar is the 5th most traded currency and the AUD/USD the 4th most traded currency pair;

Due in large part to its compulsory superannuation system, Australia has the largest pool of funds under management in the Asia-Pacific region, and the 4th largest in the world. Its primary markets are the AQUA Markets. Products and services available for trading on ASX include shares, futures, exchange traded options, warrants, contracts for difference, exchange-traded funds, real estate investment trusts, listed investment companies and interest rate securities. ASX Group has two trading platforms - ASX Trade, which facilitates the trading of ASX equity securities and ASX Trade24 for derivative securities trading.

3.3.2 The Stock Exchange in Singapore

Singapore Exchange Limited is an investment holding company located in Singapore and provides different services related to securities and derivatives trading and others. SGX is a member of the World Federation of Exchanges and the Asian and Oceanian Stock Exchanges Federation.

SGX operates several different divisions, each responsible for handling specific businesses.

- ☆ SGX ETS (Electronic Trading System): provides global trading access to SGX markets where 80 percent of the customers are from outside Singapore
- ☆ SGX DT (Derivatives Trading): provides derivatives trading
- ☆ SGX ST (Securities Trading): provides securities trading
- ☆ SGX DC (Derivatives Clearing): subsidiary for clearing and settlement operations.
- ☆ SGX Asia Clear: offers clearing services for over-the-counter (OTC) oil swaps and forward freight agreements.
- ☆ SGX Reach: an electronic trading platform.

- Central Depository Pvt Ltd: subsidiary responsible for securities clearing, settlement and depository services.
- Asian Gateway Investments Pvt Ltd: wholly owned subsidiary
- Singapore Exchange IT Solutions Pvt Ltd: provides computer services and maintenance as well as software maintenance

As of 31 December 2012, there were 776 listed companies on the Singapore Exchange with a market capitalisation of SGD 934.543 billion. The market capitalization and GDP for Australia and Singapore markets are given in Table 3.4

Table 3.4: Market Capitalization and GDP of Australia and Singapore (2000–2012)
($ US.in Millions/Billions)

Year	*Australia Market Capitalization $ USD Millions*	*Australia-GDP $ USD Billions*	*Singapore Market Capitalization $ USD Millions*	*Singapore-GDP $ USD Billions*
2000	372794	388.69	152826	86.29
2001	375130	414.98	117338	95.84
2002	378845	378.48	101900	89.29
2003	585475	394.25	229328	91.94
2004	776402	466.45	277004	97.00
2005	804073	612.87	316657	114.19
2006	1095857	693.33	276329	127.42
2007	1298429	747.20	353488	147.79
2008	675618	853.44	180021	179.98
2009	1258455	1055.03	310765	192.24
2010	1454546	926.28	370090	192.41
2011	1198163	1141.26	308320	236.42
2012	1286437	1388.06	414125	275.37

The services sector is the largest part of the Australian economy, accounting for about 70 per cent of GDP and 75 per cent of jobs. Australia was comparatively unaffected by the global financial crisis as the banking system has remained strong and inflation is under control. But the market capitalization is very low in 2008. Australia has benefited from a dramatic surge in its terms of trade in recent years, although this trend could reverse or slow due to falling global commodity prices. Australia is a significant exporter of natural resources, energy, and food. Australia's abundant and diverse natural resources attract high levels of foreign investment and include extensive reserves of coal, iron, copper, gold, natural gas, uranium, and renewable energy sources. A series of major investments, such as the US$40 billion Gorgon Liquid Natural Gas project, significantly expanded the resources sector. Australia is an open market with minimal restrictions on imports of goods and services. The process of opening up has increased productivity, stimulated growth, and made the economy more flexible and dynamic.

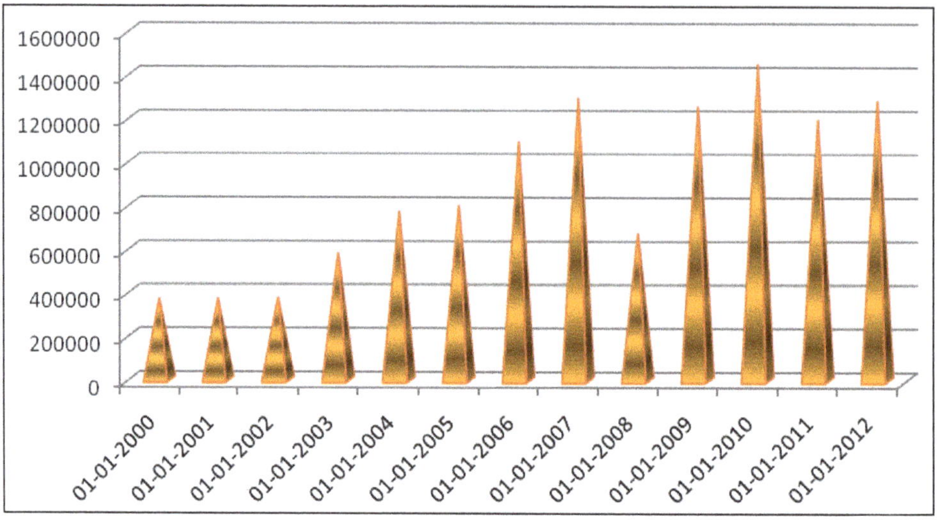

Figure 3.6: Market Capitalization in Australia Stock Exchange (2000–2014) $US Millions.

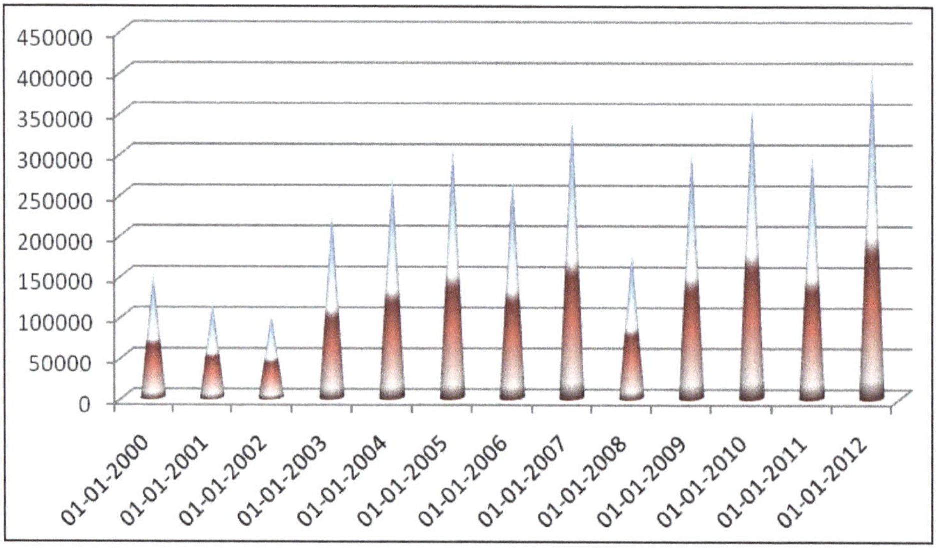

Figure 3.7: Market Capitalization in Singapore Stock Exchange (2000–2014) $US Millions.

Australia plays an active role in the World Trade Organization, APEC, the G20, and other trade forums. Australia continues to negotiate bilateral agreements with India and Indonesia, as well as larger agreements with its Pacific neighbors and the Gulf Cooperation Council countries, and an Asia-wide Regional Comprehensive Economic Partnership that includes the ten ASEAN countries and China, Japan, Korea, New Zealand and India.

Singapore has a highly developed and successful free-market economy. It enjoys a remarkably open and corruption-free environment, stable prices, and a per capita GDP higher than that of most developed countries. Unemployment is very low. The economy depends heavily on exports, particularly of consumer electronics, information technology products, medical and optical devices, pharmaceuticals, and on its vibrant transportation, business, and financial services sectors. The economy contracted 0.6 per cent in 2009 as a result of the global financial crisis, but has continued to grow since 2010 on the strength of renewed exports. The government is attempting to restructure Singapore's economy by weaning its dependence on foreign labor, addressing weak productivity, and increasing Singaporean wages. Singapore has attracted major investments in pharmaceuticals and medical technology production and will continue efforts to strengthen its position as Southeast Asia's leading financial and high-tech hub.

3.3.3 The Stock Exchange in Japan

The Tokyo Stock Exchange located in Tokyo, Japan. It is the fourth largest stock exchange in the world by aggregate market capitalization of its listed companies. Stocks listed on the TSE are separated into the First Section for large companies, the Second Section for mid-sized companies, and the others. The main index tracking the TSE is the Nikkei 225 index

3.3.4 The Stock Exchange in France

Euronext Paris is France's securities market, formerly known as the Paris Bourse, which merged with the Amsterdam, Lisbon and Brussels exchanges in September 2000 to form Euronext NV, which is the second largest exchange in Europe behind the UK'sLondon Stock Exchange. The French equities market is divided into three sections. The Premier Marché, formerly called the Official List, includes large French and foreign companies, and most Bond issues. The Second Marché, lists medium-sized companies, while Nouveau Marché lists fast-growing start up companies seeking capital to finance expansion, linked to Euro.nm, the European equity growth market. A fourth market, Marché Libre, is non regulated, administered by Euronext Paris for transactions in securities not listed on the other three markets. The CAC 40 is the exchange's benchmark, disseminated in real time.

Scarce in many natural resources, Japan has long been dependent on imported raw materials. Since the complete shutdown of Japan's nuclear reactors after the earthquake and tsunami disaster in 2011, Japan's industrial sector has become even more dependent than it was previously on imported fossil fuels. A small agricultural sector is highly subsidized and protected, with crop yields among the highest in the world. While self-sufficient in rice production, Japan imports about 60 per cent of its food on a caloric basis. Modest economic growth continued after 2000, but the economy has fallen into recession four times since 2008. Government stimulus spending helped the economy recover in late 2009 and 2010, but the economy contracted again in 2011 as the massive 9.0 magnitude earthquake and the ensuing tsunami in March of that year disrupted manufacturing. Market capitalization was very high in 2005.

Table 3.5: Market Capitalization and GDP of Japan and France (2000–2012)
($ US.in Millions/Billions)

Year	*Japan Market Capitalization $ USD Millions*	*Japan-GDP $ USD Billions*	*France Market Capitalization $ USD Millions*	*France-GDP $ USD Billions*
2000	3157221	4432.60	1446634	1500.28
2001	2251814	4731.20	1174428	1368.44
2002	2126075	4159.86	966961	1382.22
2003	3040664	3980.82	1355925	1500.34
2004	3678261	4303.94	1559109	1848.12
2005	4736512	4655.80	1758720	2124.11
2006	4726268	4571.87	2428571	2203.68
2007	4453474	4356.75	2771216	2325.01
2008	3220485	4356.35	1492327	2663.11
2009	3377892	4849.18	1972040	2923.47
2010	4099591	5055.14	1926488	2693.83
2011	3540684	5495.39	1568729	2646.99
2012	3680982	5905.65	1823339	2862.50

The French economy is diversified across all sectors. The government has partially or fully privatized many large companies, including Air France, France Telecom, Renault, and Thales. However, the government maintains a strong presence in some sectors, particularly power, public transport, and defense industries. With more than 84 million foreign tourists per year, France is the most visited country in the world and maintains the third largest income in the world from tourism.

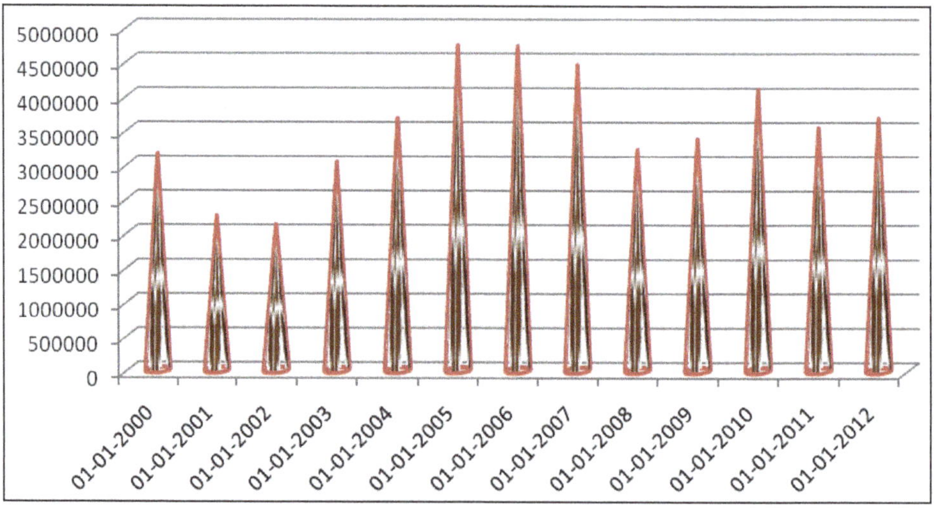

Figure 3.8: Market Capitalization in Japan Stock Exchange (2000–2014) $US Millions.

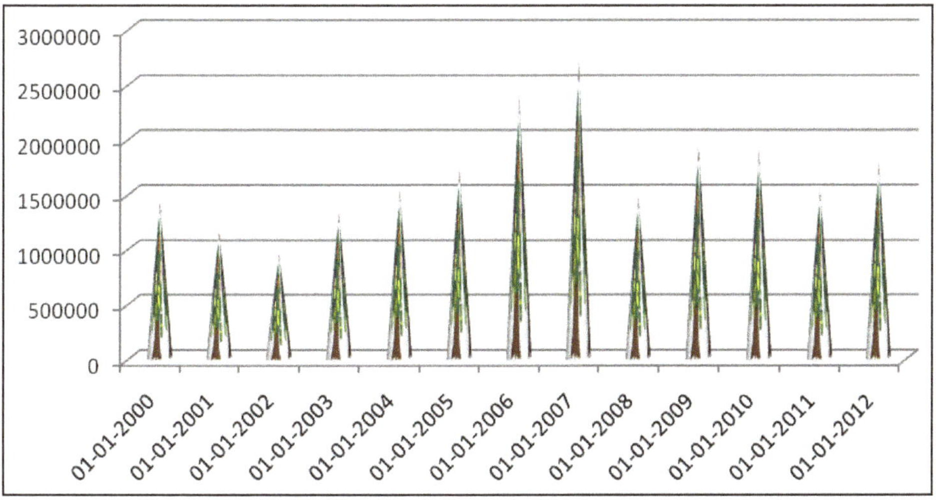

Figure 3.9: Market Capitalization in France Stock Exchange (2000–2014) $US Millions.

The unemployment rate (including overseas territories) increased from 7.8 per cent in 2008 to 10.4 per cent in the fourth quarter of 2014. Youth unemployment in metropolitan France decreased from a high of 25.4 per cent in the fourth quarter of 2012. The budget deficit rose sharply from 3.3 per cent of GDP in 2008 to 7.5 per cent of GDP in 2009. Market capitalisation was very high in 2007.

3.3.5 The Stock Exchange in Germany

The Frankfurt Stock Exchange is the world's 10th largest stock exchange by market capitalization. Located in Frankfurt, Germany, the Frankfurt Stock Exchange is owned and operated by Deutsche Börse which also owns the European futures exchange Eurex and the clearing company Clear stream. It is located in the district of Innenstadt and within the central business district known as Bankenviertel.

The Frankfurt Stock Exchange accounts for over 90 percent of the turnover in the German market and a very large share of the European market. The Frankfurt Stock Exchange has more than 250 international trading institutions and more than 4,500 traders. Investors directly connected to the Frankfurt Stock Exchange represent 35 per cent of the world's investment capital.

3.3.6 The Stock Exchange in Hong Kong

The Hong Kong (HKEx) is a Chinese stock exchange located in Hong Kong. It is Asia's third largest stock exchange in terms of market capitalization behind the Tokyo Stock Exchange and Shanghai Stock Exchange, and the sixth largest in the world behind Euronext. In 1891 it was established as an Association of Stockbrokers of Hong Kong. Later it was renamed as The Hong Kong Stock Exchange in 1914.

The market infrastructure of the exchange was much improved with the introduction of the Central Clearing and Settlement System (CCASS) in June 1992 and the Automatic Order Matching and Execution System (AMS) in November

1993. The third generation of the trading system, AMS/3, was launched in 2000. It provides enhanced functionality and a platform for a straight-through transaction process. The market capitalization and GDP for Germany and Hong-Kong markets are given in Table 3.6

Table 3.6: Market Capitalisation and GDP for Germany and Hong Kong (2000–2012) ($ US.in Millions/Billions)

Year	*Germany Market Capitalization $ USD Millions*	*Germany-GDP $ USD Billions*	*Hong Kong Market Capitalization $ USD Millions*	*Hong Kong-GDP $ USD Billions*
2000	127024	2196.69	623397	165.77
2001	107174	1947.21	506072	171.67
2002	691124	1947.93	463084	169.40
2003	107902	2076.30	551236	166.35
2004	119451	2502.31	665248	161.38
2005	122125	2815.47	693486	169.10
2006	163782	2857.63	895249	181.57
2007	210550	2998.62	1162565	193.54
2008	110795	3435.68	1328837	211.60
2009	129756	3746.92	915825	219.28
2010	142970	3412.98	1079640	214.05
2011	118445	3412.21	889596	228.64
2012	148631	3751.88	1108127	248.51

The German economy - the fifth largest economy in the world in PPP terms and Europe's largest - is a leading exporter of machinery, vehicles, chemicals, and household equipment and benefits from a highly skilled labor force. Like its

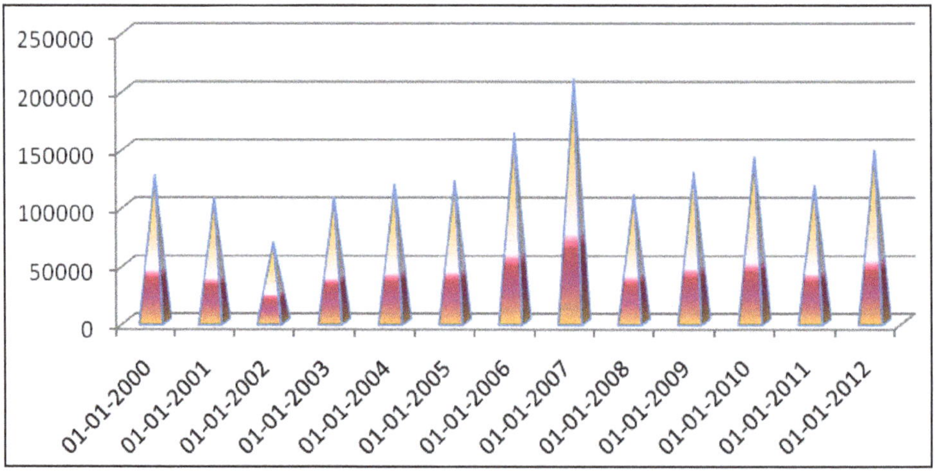

Figure 3.10: Market Capitalization in Germany Stock Exchange (2000–2014) $US Millions.

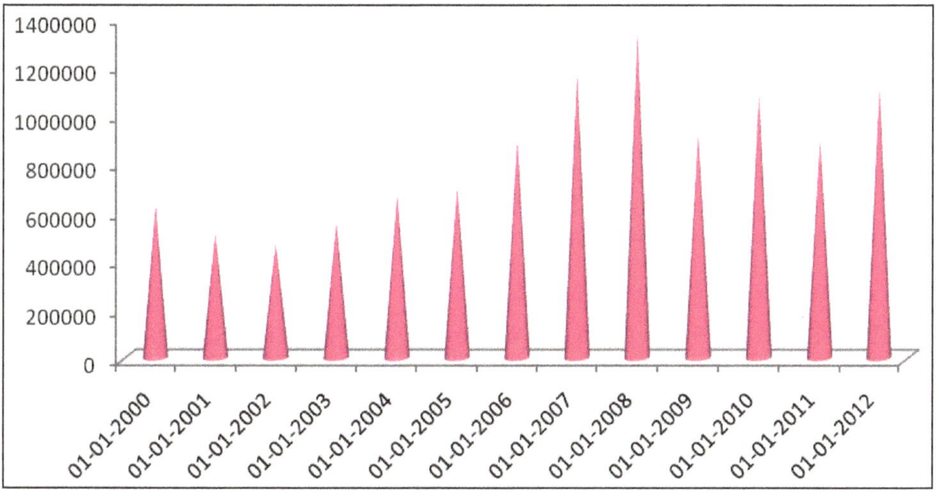

Figure 3.11: Market Capitalization in Hong Kong Stock Exchange (2000–2014) $US Millions.

Western European neighbors, Germany faces significant demographic challenges to sustained long-term growth. Low fertility rates and declining net immigration are increasing pressure on the country's social welfare system and necessitate structural reforms. Reforms launched by the government of Chancellor Gerhard SCHROEDER (1998-2005), deemed necessary to address chronically high unemployment and low average growth, contributed to strong growth and falling unemployment. These advances, as well as a government subsidized, reduced working hour scheme, help explain the relatively modest increase in unemployment during the 2008-09 recession - the deepest since World War II. Stimulus and stabilization efforts initiated in 2008 and 2009 and tax cuts introduced in Chancellor Angela MERKEL's second term increased Germany's total budget deficit - including federal, state, and municipal - to 4.1 per cent in 2010, but slower spending and higher tax revenues reduced the deficit to 0.8 per cent in 2011 and in 2012 A constitutional amendment approved in 2009 limits the federal government to structural deficits of no more than 0.35 per cent of GDP per annum as of 2016 though the target was already reached in 2012. Market capitalization reached its peak in the year 2007. Following the March 2011 Fukushima nuclear disaster, has plummeted the market.

Hong Kong has a free market economy, highly dependent on international trade and finance - the value of goods and services trade, including the sizable share of re-exports, is about four times GDP. Hong Kong has no tariffs on imported goods, and it levies excise duties on only four commodities, whether imported or produced locally: hard alcohol, tobacco, hydrocarbon oil, and methyl alcohol. There are no quotas or dumping laws. Hong Kong's open economy left it exposed to the global economic slowdown that began in 2008. Although increasing integration with China, through trade, tourism, and financial links, helped it to make an initial recovery more quickly than many observers anticipated, its continued reliance on foreign trade and investment leaves it vulnerable to renewed global financial market volatility or a slowdown in the global economy. The Hong Kong government is promoting the Special Administrative Region (SAR) as the site for Chinese renminbi (RMB) internationalization. Hong Kong residents are allowed to establish RMB-denominated savings accounts; RMB-denominated corporate and Chinese government bonds have been issued in Hong Kong; and RMB trade settlement is allowed. The territory far exceeded the RMB conversion quota set by Beijing for trade settlements in 2010 due to the growth of earnings from exports to the mainland. Market capitalization was again low in the year 2011.

3.3.7 The Stock Exchange in US

The **NASDAQ Stock Market is** commonly known as the NASDAQ (currently stylized as Nasdaq), is an American/Canadian stock exchange. It is the second-largest exchange in the world by market capitalization, behind only the New York Stock Exchange. In 1972, NASDAQ stood for National Association of Securities Dealers Automated Quotations. NASDAQ was founded in 1971 by the National Association of Securities Dealers (NASD), which divested itself of NASDAQ in a series of sales in 2000 and 2001. NASDAQ is owned and operated by the NASDAQ OMX Group, the stocks of which were listed on its own stock exchange beginning July 2, 2002, under the ticker symbol NDAQ. It was the world's first electronic stock market. At first, it was merely a *quotation system* and did not provide a way to perform electronic trades. The National Association of Securities Dealers turned NASDAQ in 2000 to form a publicly traded company, the NASDAQ Stock Market, Inc. In 2006, the status of NASDAQ was changed from a stock market to a licensed national securities exchange.

3.3.8 The Stock Exchange in UK

The **London Stock Exchange** is located in the City of London in the United Kingdom. The Exchange was founded in 1801 and its current premises are situated in Paternoster Square close to St Paul's Cathedral in the City of London. The Exchange is part of the London Stock Exchange Group. FTSE 100 Index turned out to be one of the most useful indices of all and tracked the movements of the 100 leading companies listed on the Exchange.

International companies can list a number of products in London including shares, depositary receipts and debt, offering different and cost-effective ways to raise capital. In 2004 the Exchange opened a Hong Kong office and has attracted more than 200 companies from the Asia-Pacific region.

The securities available for trading on the London Stock Exchange:

- Bonds, including retail bonds
- Covered warrants
- Exchange-traded products
- Exchange-traded funds
- Global depositary receipts (GDRs)
- Common stock
- Structured products

There are currently 2,938 companies from over 60 countries listed on the London Stock Exchange, of which 1151 are on AIM, 44 on the Professional Securities Market and 10 on the Specialist Funds Market. The market capitalization and GDP for US and UK markets are given in Table 3.7

Table 3.7: Market Capitalisation and GDP for US and UK (2000–2012)

($ US.in Millions/Billions)

Year	*UK Market Capitalization $ USD Millions*	*UK-GDP $ USD Billions*	*US Market Capitalization $ USD Millions*	*US-GDP $ USD Billions*
2000	151040	9660.60	2576991	1558.32
2001	138546	10284.8	2164716	1548.66
2002	110981	10621.8	1864262	1529.09
2003	142662	10977.50	2460063	1674.42
2004	163237	11510.7	2815928	1943.71
2005	169708	12274.1	3058182	2298.04
2006	194258	13091.7	3794310	2412.11
2007	199472	13655.9	3858505	2582.75
2008	117376	14477.60	1851953	2963.10
2009	150772	14718.60	2796444	2791.68
2010	171389	14418.70	3107037	2309.00
2011	156407	14964.40	2903178	2407.68
2012	186683	15517.90	3019467	2592.02

The US has the most technologically powerful economy in the world, with a per capita GDP of $54,800. US firms are at or near the forefront in technological advances, especially in computers, pharmaceuticals, and medical, aerospace, and military equipment; however, their advantage has narrowed since the end of

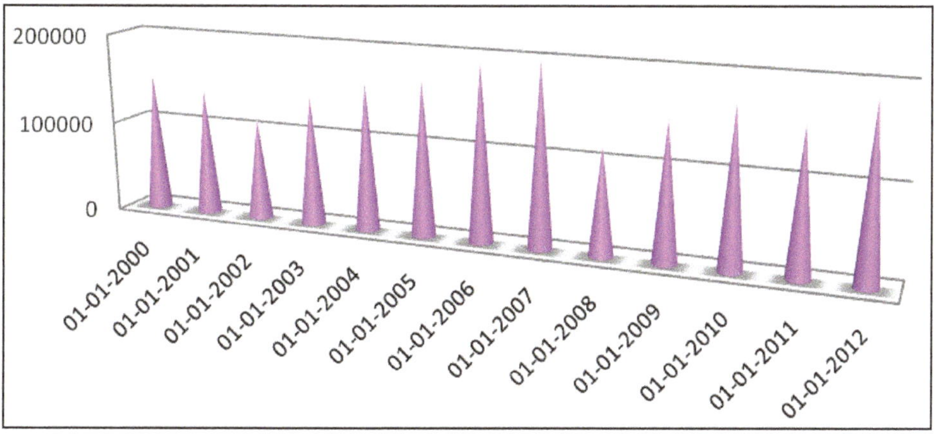

Figure 3.12: Market Capitalization in US Stock Exchange (2000–2014) $US Millions.

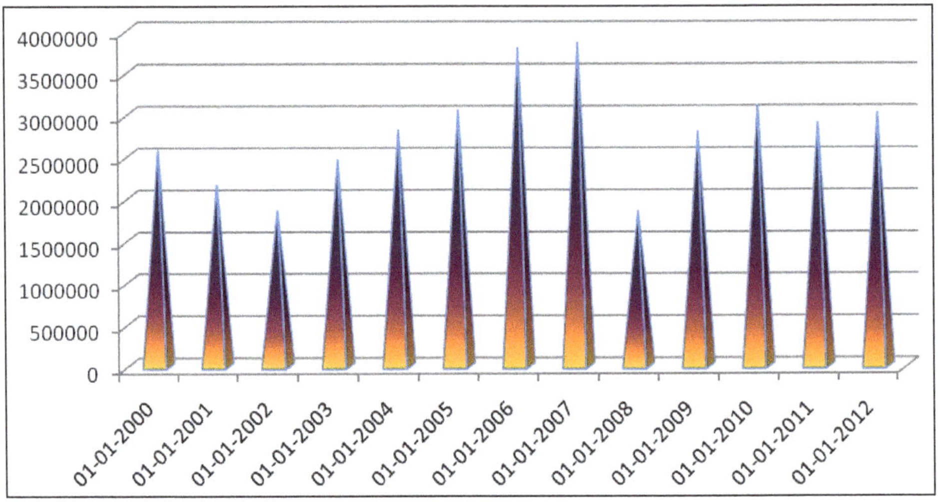

Figure 3.13: Market Capitalization in UK Stock Exchange (2000–2014) $US Millions.

World War II. In the US, private individuals and business firms make most of the decisions, and the federal and state governments buy needed goods and services predominantly in the private marketplace. US business firms enjoy greater flexibility than their counterparts in Western Europe and Japan in decisions to expand capital plant, to lay off surplus workers, and to develop new products. At the same time, they face higher barriers to enter their rivals' home markets than foreign firms face entering US markets.

The globalization of trade, and especially the rise of low-wage producers such as China, has put additional downward pressure on wages and upward pressure on the return to capital. Crude oil prices doubled between 2001 and 2006, the year home prices peaked; higher gasoline prices ate into consumers' budgets and many individuals fell behind in their mortgage payments. Oil prices climbed another 50 per cent between 2006 and 2008, and bank foreclosures more than doubled in the same period. Besides dampening the housing market, soaring oil prices caused a drop in the value of the dollar and deterioration in the US merchandise trade deficit, which peaked at $840 billion in 2008

The sub-prime mortgage crisis, falling home prices, investment bank failures, tight credit, and the global economic downturn pushed the United States into a recession by mid-2008. GDP contracted until the third quarter of 2009, making this the deepest and longest downturn since the Great Depression. To help stabilize financial markets, the US Congress established a $700 billion Troubled Asset Relief Program (TARP) in October 2008. The government used some of these funds to purchase equity in US banks and industrial corporations, much of which had been returned to the government by early 2011. In 2010 and 2011, the federal budget deficit reached nearly 9 per cent of GDP. In 2012, the federal government reduced the growth of spending and the deficit shrank to 7.6 per cent of GDP. Wars in Iraq and Afghanistan required major shifts in national resources from civilian to military purposes and contributed to the growth of the budget deficit and public debt.

In UK following the 2008-09 global economic crisis, the EU economy saw moderate GDP growth in 2010 and 2011 but has struggled since the sovereign debt crisis in the euro zone intensified in 2011. Despite EU/IMF rescue programs in Greece, Ireland, Portugal, Spain and Cyprus, significant drags on growth remain, including high public and private debt loads, low domestic demand that discourages investment, aging populations, onerous regulations, and high unemployment. Market capitalization was very low in the year 2008.

3.4 Analysis of GDP Growth Trend

Gross Domestic Product (GDP) is one of the most widely used measures of an economy's output or production. It is defined as the total value of goods and services produced within a country's borders in a specific time period – monthly, quarterly or annually.GDP is an accurate indication of an economy's size, while GDP per capita has a close correlation with t he trend in living standards over time, and the GDP growth rate is probably the single best indicator of economic growth.

For analyzing growth trend of market capitalization and GDP, regression is used to estimate the linear growth, compound growth, cubic growth and quadratic growth. By evaluating performance trends, corporate analysts also can tell whether an organization is adeptly managing its money and investing it wisely.

3.5 Growth Trend

It is estimated with the help of the following formulas:

Linear Growth Y = b0 + (b1 * t).

Compound Growth Y = b0 * (b1**t)

Quadratic Growth Y = b0 + (b1 * t) + (b2 * t**2).

Table 3.8: Growth Trend in Developing Countries (Market Capitalization 2000–2012)

Particulars	*Growth Function*	α	β^1	R^2
CHINA	Linear	445479.85 (4.247)	55946.42 (4.233)*	0.620
	Compound	480256.122 (8.325)	1.075 (66.075)*	0.672
INDONESIA	Linear	–692564.57 (–1.918)	355747.28 (7.161)*	0.823
	Compound	18234.34 (5.890)	1.283 (46.572)*	0.925
MALAYSIA	Linear	49735.58 (1.582)	27910.58 (7.048)*	0.819
	Compound	98215.43 (9.625)	1.122 (76.394)*	0.876
KOREA	Linear	77013.76 (0.740)	84290.48 (6.432)*	0.790

Contd...

Table 3.8–*Contd...*

Particulars	Growth Function	α	β[1]	R^2
	Compound	185241.22 (5.599)	1.170 (44.437)*	0.815
INDIA	Linear	–65543.61 (–0.313)	118887.98 (4.501)*	0.648
	Compound	112717.06 (3.695)	1.250 (29.325)*	0.795

t values are significant at 5 per cent level. Figures in the parenthesis are t value.

Table 3.9: Growth Trend in Developed Countries (Market Capitalization 2000–2012)

Particulars	Growth Function	α	β[1]	R^2
AUSTRALIA	Linear	265726.06 (2.299)	89074.47 (6.116)*	0.773
	Compound	353875.08 (6.850)	1.123 (54.371)*	0.783
SINGAPORE	Linear	120528.20 (3.281)	20234.28 (4.372)*	0.635
	Compound	129848.27 (5.677)	1.093 (45.057)*	0.592
JAPAN	Linear	2880222.00 (6.337)	95022.38 (1.659)*	0.247
	Compound	270069.31 (7.506)	1.032 (59.575)*	0.247
FRANCE	Linear	1295840.53 (4.863)	59324.83 (1.767)*	0.221
	Compound	1255717.70 (6.810)	1.040 (54.054)*	0.287
GERMANY	Linear	248823.15 (2.666)	–10274.41 (–0.874)*	0.065
	Compound	173667.01 (3.318)	0.979 (26.336)*	0.028
HONG-kONG	Linear	445479.84 (4.247)	55946.41 (4.233)*	0.649
	Compound	480256.12 (8.325)	1.075 (66.078)*	0.672
US	Linear	138380.57 (9.089)	2786.63 (1.453)*	0.161
	Compound	137191.09 (9.956)	1.018 (79.021)*	
UK	Linear	2359318.84 (6.665)	61537.26 (1.380)*	0.148
	Compound	2314195.72 (7.683)	1.024 (60.979)*	0.155

t values are significant at 5 per cent level. Figures in the parenthesis are t value.

All the countries market capitalization has experienced both linear and compound growth trend.

Table 3.10: GDP Growth Trend in Developing Countries

Particulars	*Growth Function*	α	β^1	R^2
CHINA	Linear	–0.408.383 (–0.942)	501.966 (9.188)*	0.885
	Compound	795.095 (18.623)	1.181 (147.812)*	0.982
INDONESIA	Linear	–21.712 (–0.426)	57.314 (8.928)*	0.879
	Compound	108.852 (20.975)	1.166 (166.487)*	0.994
MALAYSIA	Linear	42.008 (3.930)	16.743 (12.433)*	0.934
	Compound	69.124 (24.019)	1.113 (190.646)*	0.974
KOREA	Linear	422.714 (8.153)	59.052 (9.040)*	0.881
	Compound	473.983 (15.642)	1.078 (124.154)*	0.887
INDIA	Linear	132.106 (1.714)	117.932 (12.145)*	0.931
	Compound	353.590 (21.914)	1.134 (173.939)*	0.934
TAIWAN	Linear	269.625 (22.713)	12.867 (8.063)*	0.871
	Compound	277.905 (31.462)	1.036 (249.720)*	0.877

t values are significant at 5 per cent level. Figures in the parenthesis are t value

Table 3.11: GDP Growth Trend in Developed Countries

Particulars	*Growth Function*	α	β^1	R^2
AUSTRALIA	Linear	161.988 (2.759)	80.821 (10.927)*	0.916
	Compound	299.495 (15.758)	1.120 (125.079)*	0.948
SINGAPORE	Linear	42.386 (3.479)	15.112 (9.845)*	0.898
	Compound	68.016 (17.340)	1.106 (137.635)*	0.945
JAPAN	Linear	3963.765 (17.605)	102.479 (3.612)*	0.543
	Compound	4021.112 (21.561)	1.021 (171.137)*	0.537

Contd...

Table 3.11–*Contd...*

Particulars	*Growth Function*	α	β^1	R^2
FRANCE	Linear	1160.439 (10.452)	142.378 (10.179)*	0.904
	Compound	1277.645 (17.129)	1.072 (135.959)*	0.891
GERMANY	Linear	1716.368 (12.648)	162.517 (9.506)*	0.891
	Compound	1838.953 (19.093)	1.061 (151.542)*	0.879
HONG-KONG	Linear	144.545 (21.075)	6.833 (7.907)*	0.850
	Compound	149.456 (29.442)	1.035 (233.688)*	0.856
US	Linear	9233.858 (43.825)	506.969 (19.098)*	0.971
	Compound	9509.054 (52.567)	1.041 (417.238)*	0.963
UK	Linear	1458.806 (8.549)	106.001 (4.931)*	0.688
	Compound	1494.948 (12.946)	1.053 (102.753)*	0.718

The entire Capital market segment has experienced both linear and compound growth trend. All the countries experienced linear and compound tren in the GDP growth.

Conclusion

The market capitalization of all the countries was very low in the year 2008 due to global financial crisis except China and Hong Kong. In China and Hong Kong it vas very low in 2009. The effect of global financial crisis was reflected in the year 2009. Among all the countries China GDP was very high among the developing countries. US GDP was very high among all the countries selected for the study. All the markets' market capitalization and GDP experienced linear and compund growth trend. It is a good sign for the market that market is growing sifnificantly. From 2008 – 2012 US, China, India, Japan and Germany GDP PPP occupied first, second, third, fourth and fifthe rank respectively.

References

1. *"History of ASX". Australian Securities Exchange. Retrieved 18 April 2011.*
2. *"Headlights on trading and investment". "APSEC".*Australian Securities Exchange. Retrieved 19 May 2011.
3. *"Guide to Equity Options for Investment Managers" (PDF).*

4. *"History of the Frankfurt Stock Exchange – Fairs, coins and bills of exchange: 11th - 17th century". Deutsche Börse. Retrieved 9 July 2015*
5. http://www.boerse-frankfurt.de/en/start
6. http://www.hkex.com.hk/eng/listing/listhk/our_markets.htm
7. https://www.hkex.com.hk/eng/stat/epstat/floorstat/2014floorstat.htm
8. http://www.thejakartapost.*com/news/ "IDX will start trading day earlier in January". 2 November 2012.*
9. http://www.thejakartapost.*com/news "IDX unveils ways to be SE Asia's largest stock market". 13 February 2012.*
10. http://www.sseinitiative.org/fact-sheet/krx/. *"Korea Exchange". Sustainable Stock Exchanges Initiative. Retrieved 14 May 2015.*
11. Market Hours, Korea Exchange via Wikinvest
12. http://www.atimes.com/se-asia/ *"INVESTMENT IN MALAYSIA". Asia Times. Retrieved 10 December 2012.*
13. http://www.nytimes/2000-01-01 *"INTERNATIONAL BUSINESS; Malaysia Extends Deadline in Singapore Exchange Dispute". New York Times. 1 January 2000. Retrieved 10 December 2012.*
14. http://www.economies.com/node *"Malaysia's stockmarket; Daylight Robbery". The Economist. 10 July 1999. Retrieved 10*
15. http://www.investopedia.com/terms/m/marketcapitalization.asp#ixzz3p08PTgT3 Market Capitalization Definition | Investopedia
16. http://www,londonstockexchange.com/ Monthly Market Report - London Stock Exchange
17. http://www.computerweekly.com *"London Stock Exchange to replace Tradelect with Millennium". London: ComputerWeekly.com. 4 September 2009.*
18. http://www.telegraph.co.uk/finance/markets *Rowena Mason (10 September 2008). "Seven-hour LSE blackout caused by double glitch". London: The Telegraph.*
19. http://www.bbc.co.uk *"London Stock Exchange trading hit by technical glitch". BBC News. 26 November 2009.*
20. http://www.itwire.com *David M. Williams (8 October 2009). "London Stock Exchange gets the facts and dumps Windows for Linux". ITWire.*
21. http://www.china-briefing.com/news China Briefing - Foreigners Now Allowed to List on Shanghai Stock Exchange retrieved on January 21, 2009.
22. http://www.msnab.msn/id/ MSNBC - China shares tumble as panic spreads - retrieved on June 4, 2007.
23. Market Hours, Shanghai Stock Exchange via Wikinvest
24. Market Hours, Taiwan Stock Exchange via Wikinvest
25. *The Economic Times. June 19, 2010. Retrieved 19 Jun 2010*

26. Market Hours, Tokyo Securities Exchange via Wikinvest

27. *Singapore Exchange Ltd. Summary Annual Report 2008 (PDF), Singapore Exchange Ltd., p. 9*

28. http://www.gfrlaw.com/pubs/. *"Nasdaq Stock Market Becomes A National Securities Exchange; Changes Market Designations".*

Chapter 4

Market Efficiency of the International Stock Markets

4.1 Introduction

Informational efficiency of the markets invites the substantial attention of the financial scholars and practitioners. The understanding of the efficiency of the stock markets becomes imperative because of the increased flow of investments across international boundaries due to the integration of world economies. It is assumed to be an important concept for an extensive understanding of the capital markets. Stock market efficiency portrays the functioning of capital markets and their performance and contribution to the development of a country's economy. Market efficiency is used to explain the association between the information and share prices in the market. Market efficiency influences the investment strategy of an investor because, if the market is efficient, then trying to pick up winners will be mere wastage of time. On the other hand, if markets are not efficient, excess returns can be earned by correctly picking the winners. Traditionally more developed Western equity markets are considered to be more efficient.

In the last two decades, many emerging markets had initiated reform process to open up their economies. In the recent past, emerging markets have attracted foreign investment and became viable alternative for investors seeking international diversification. At present, thousands of intelligent, affluent, and well-educated investors are in the securities markets and they are interested in buying underpriced securities and selling over-priced securities.

In the 'efficient' market important current information will be freely available to all participants and enable them to predict future market values of individual securities. The efficient market hypothesis is related to the random walk theory. Bachelier in 1900 (Poshakwale 1996)[1] expounded the concept that asset prices may follow a random walk pattern. The random walk hypothesis explains that the successive price changes are independent of each other. In other words, in an efficient market at any point of time the actual price of a security will be a good estimate of its intrinsic value. (Eugene F. Fama 1965)[2]. The efficiency of the markets depends on the extent of absorption of information, the time taken for absorption and the type of information absorbed. Fama (1970)[3] has first introduced the notion of capital market efficiency. Fama (1991)[4] categorized market efficiency into three forms - weak, semi-strong and strong.

Weak-Form Efficiency

when a market is weak form efficient, equity returns are not serially correlated and a mean is not constant. If the market is weak form efficient, security prices will reflect all the relevant information at any time and a trading rule based on the past prices will not be useful to identify mispriced assets. This form claims that any attempt to predict prices based on historical information are totally futile as future price changes are independent of past price changes. In the weak form efficient market, investors can not earn abnormal profits by planning out a trading rule based solely on past price models.

Semi-strong Form Efficiency

A market is semi - strong efficient if stock prices instantaneously reflect any new publicly available information. In this market securities are neither undervalued nor are overvalued hence trading rules incapable of producing higher returns. When new information is released, it is fully incorporated into the price rather speedily. In other words, fundamental analysis is of no use.

Strong-Form Efficiency

In the strong form efficiency all available information, even private information will be reflected in the security prices. Hence, the strong form does not hold in a world with an uneven playing field.

For the investors the Hypothesis of Market Efficiency is an important concept to diversify their investment in various portfolios. Efficient Market Hypothesis proposes that share price changes are unpredictable, i.e random. The Weak Form Efficient Market Hypothesis examines whether past series of share prices are useful in predicting the future share price or not. The more the investors and the quicker the dissemination of information, the more efficient a market should be. The lower the market efficiency, the greater will be the predictability of stock price changes. In an efficient market, information is freely available and the prices of the shares approximate to its intrinsic value. Successive price changes will be dependent if there is the gradual flow of new information. However, successive price changes will be random if the adjustment to information is almost immediate. Thus, price movements in a weak-form efficient market occur randomly and successive price changes are independent of one another.[5] This test measures the statistical dependence between price changes. If there is no dependence between the past prices and the future prices (*i.e.*, price changes are random), then the market supports Weak Form Efficient Hypothesis.

The empirical research on market efficiency has been done, in two broad categories, namely technical analysis and fundamental analysis. Technical analysis is used to examine the weak form efficient market hypothesis. The other is fundamental analysis, which assumes that factors other than past security prices are relevant in the determination of the future prices. The Weak Form Efficient Market Hypothesis can be examined into two sub- approaches: one is to determine the existence of predictability using past return series or price information. Another is to use technical trading rules if they can be exploited as profit making strategy.[6]

Voluminous literature is available on studying the behavior of the stock price over time. The results of the previous research proved that the markets of developed countries are weak form efficient. That means the successive returns are independent and follow the random walk. In case of emerging markets there are two findings. One group of researchers have supported weak form efficiency in emerging countries and while others rejected the weak form efficiency in emerging markets..

Studies on the developed market supported the weak-form efficiency of the market on the basis of low degree of serial correlation and transaction cost (Working, 1934[7]; Kendall, 1943[8], 1953[9]; Cootner, 1962[10]; Osborne, 1962[11]; Fama, 1965[12]). Groenewold and Kang (1993)[13], Narayan and Smyth (2005)[14]. All of the studies supported the EMH that price changes are random and past changes were not useful in forecasting future price changes particularly after transaction costs were taken into account. Overall, the empirical studies on developed market sustain the weak-form efficiency of the EMH in general.

However, some other studies which rejected weak form efficiency in the developed markets are Fama and French, (1988)[15]; Poterba and Summers, (1988)[16] Hudson, Dempsey and Keasey (1994)[17] Kwan Sim, Cotsomitis (1995)[18] Nicolaas, (1997)[19]

Though it is generally believed that the emerging markets are less efficient, the empirical evidence does not always support the notion. There are two groups of findings; the first group substantiates weak-form efficiency in developing and less developed markets. They are Branes, 1986[20], (on the Kuala Lumpur Stock Exchange); Chan, Gup and Pan, 1992[21], (in major Asian markets) ; Dickinson and Muragu, 1994[22] (on the Nairobi Stock Exchange) and Ojah and Karemera 1999[23], (on the four Latin American countries market) Amanulla S. and Kamaiah.B 1997[24] (Indian stock market). Ramasastri A.S. 2000[25] (Indian stock markets) Pradhan H.K. and Lakshmi S. Narasimhan 2002[26] (Indian stock market) Hasan 2004[27] (Dhaka Stock Exchange). The estimated results show that the null hypothesis of randomness cannot be rejected and stock prices have a significant random walk or permanent component.

Whereas the others reject the weak-form efficiency in the developing and emerging markets are Roux and Gilberson 1978[28] (Johannesburg stock exchange) Claessens, Dasgupta and Glen 1995[29], (emerging markets) Sunil Poshakwale 1996[30] (Indian stock market) Nourrrendine Khaba 1998[31] (Saudi Financial market) Madhusoodanan 1998[32] (India stock market) Asma Mobarek and Kevin Keasey, 2000[33] (Dhaka Stock Exchange) Hyun-Jung Ryoo and Graham Smith 2000[34] (Korean stock market) Sarath P. Abeysekera 2001[35] (Colombo Stock Exchange) Sunil

Poshakwale 2002[36] (Indian market). Chaudhuri and Wu (2003)[37] Ibrahim Awad and Zahran Daraghma (2009)[38]

This study considers both traditional tests (such as, Kolmogorov Smirnov Goodness of Fit, Run test, Autocorrelation test and Ljung Box test) and dynamic time series model (such as Dicky Fuller and Augmented Dicky Fuller model) which perhaps claims better findings.

4.2 Non Parametric Tests

4.2.1 Kolmogorov Smirnov Goodness of Fit Test

Kolmogorov Smirnov Goodness of Fit Test (KS) is a non –parametric test and is used to determine how well a random sample of data fits a particular distribution (normal).. It compares the observed cumulative distribution function for a variable with a specified theoretical distribution which may be normal, uniform, Poisson, or exponential. The KS one sample test goodness of fit test compares the cumulative distribution function for variable with a uniform or normal distributions and tests whether the distributions are homogeneous. It checks whether the observations have come from the specified distribution. Normal parameters are used to test distribution.

The Kolmogorov-Smirnov test statistic is defined as[39]

$$D = \max_{1 \leq i \leq N} \left(F(Y_i) - \frac{i-1}{N}, \frac{i}{N} - F(Y_i) \right)$$

where *F* is the theoretical cumulative distribution of the distribution being tested which must be a continuous distribution (*i.e.*, no discrete distributions such as the binomial or Poisson), and it must be fully specified (*i.e.*, the location, scale, and shape parameters cannot be estimated from the data). The computed Z is compared to a table of critical values of Z in the One-Sample Kolmogorov-Smirnov Goodness-of-Fit Test, for a given sample size.

The hypothesis for this test is shown as the following;

H_0: The data follow a normal distribution

H_a: The data do not follow the normal distribution

4.2.2 The Runs Analysis

The run test is another approach to detect the statistical independencies which means randomness. A run is a sequence of consecutive positive or negative returns. By comparing the total number of runs in the data with the expected number of runs under random walk hypothesis, the test of the random walk hypothesis may be constructed. To perform the test, the sampling distribution of the total number of runs in a sample is required. The r –statistic follows a normal distribution with a mean and standard deviation given by the following formulae[40].

$$\mu(r_i) = 2n_1n_2/(n_1 + n_2) + 1$$

$$\sigma(r_i) = \sqrt{2n_1n_2(2n_1n_2 - n_1n_2)/(n_1+n_2)^2(n_1+n_2-1)}$$

This test is performed by examining a time series of returns for a security and testing whether the number of consecutive price gains or drops shows a pattern. A price gain is represented by a " +", a price drop is represented by a "- " and "0" shows that return is zero. The run test converts the total number of runs into a Z statistic. For large samples the Z statistics gives the probability of difference between actual and expected number of runs. The Z values is greater than or equal to 1.96, then the null hypothesis that stock returns follow random walk is rejected. The null hypothesis is that stock returns depict a random walk through time. If the absolute value of Z is greater than Z critical value 1.96 for =0.05)

Our hypothesis for run test shown as the following;

H0: Price changes are random.

H1: Price changes are not random.

The results of Kolmogorov Smirnov Goodness of Fit Test and Runs test are given in Tables 4.1 and 4.2 for the whole study period..

Table 4.1: Estimates of Kolmogorov Smirnov Goodness of Fit Test for Daily Returns (2000–2012)

Countries	*Absolute*	*Positive*	*Negative*	*K-S Z*	*Z-Tailed P*
China	0.088	0.088	–0.036	4.753*	0.000
Indonesia	0.135	0.135	–0.079	6.580*	0.000
KolaLumpur	0.103	0.103	–0.100	5.627*	0.000
Korea	0.113	0.085	–0.113	5.627*	0.000
India	0.132	0.098	–0.132	7.200*	0.000
Taiwan	0.090	0.038	–0.090	4.902*	0.000
Australia	0.162	0.162	–0.079	8.055*	0.000
Singapore	0.090	0.054	–0.090	4.951*	0.000
Japan	0.091	0.091	–0.083	4.941*	0.000
France	0.073	0.073	–0.054	4.069*	0.000
Germany	0.100	0.060	–0.100	5.546*	0.000
Hong Kong	0.080	0.046	–0.080	4.520*	0.000
US	0.072	0.072	–0.070	3.955*	0.000
UK	0.082	0.062	–0.082	4.521*	0.000

* Significant at 5 per cent level.

The data for 14 stock market indices namely USA, (Nasdaq) UK, (FTSE), Germany (Dax) France (CAC 40), Singapore,(STI), Australia, (AORD), Japan (Nikkei) Hong – Kong (Hang Seng) China (SSEC), Indonesia (JKSE), Kola Lumpur (KLSE), Korea (KS11), Taiwan (TWII) and India (Nifty) are considered. The daily adjusted closing stock prices of these indices are gathered since April 2000 to March 2012 for empirical analysis. To confirm the distribution pattern of the stock return series,

Kolmogorov Smirnov Goodness of Fit Test is used, which provides evidence, whether the distribution confirm to a normal distribution or not. In the first step of empirical analysis, the results of Kolmogorov Smirnov Goodness of Fit Test and Run test are briefly reported in the Tables 4.1 and 4.2, which provide some statistical information about the stock prices of each country.

Table 4.2: Runs Test for Daily Returns (2000–2012)

Countries	*Total Runs*	*Z*	*2-Tailed P*
China	30	–52.935*	0.000
Indonesia	22	–47.642*	0.000
Kola Lumpur	39	–52.990*	0.000
Korea	22	–51.260*	0.000
India	26	–53.813*	0.000
Taiwan	37	–53.382*	0.000
Australia	18	–49.066*	0.000
Singapore	20	–54.281*	0.000
Japan	48	–52.526*	0.000
France	58	–53.340*	0.000
Germany	73	–52.704*	0.000
Hong Kong	45	–55.076*	0.000
US	65	–52.615*	0.000
UK	65	–52.729*	0.000

* Significant at 5 per cent level.

Results from the Table 4.1 Kolmogorov Smirnov Goodness of Fit Test (K-S test) show 0.000 probabilities for the Z at the 5 per cent level of significance, in case of normal distribution. The results clearly indicate that the frequency distribution of the daily values of the stock price index do not fit normal distribution. The embodied result reveals that the null hypothesis of the random walk could not be accepted for the stock price of various countries.

Table 4.2 clearly states that the Z statistics of daily market return is greater than 1.96 and negative for all the countries which means that the observed number of runs is fewer than the expected number of runs with observed significance level and it indicates that the series return are not following the random walk model. Therefore, null hypothesis of independence is rejected at a 5 per cent level. Thus we conclude that all the countries are non-random, implying that the test fails to support weak form efficiency.

4.3 Parametric Tests

The study investigates the parametric tests to examine whether the finding of non-parametric test is confirmed by the findings of parametric tests or not. The extent of dependency is also measured with the parameters estimated under different statistical techniques.

4.3.1 Autocorrelation Test ACF(k)

The autocorrelation coefficient provides a measure of the relationship between the value of a random variable in time t (x_t) and its value at k periods earlier (x_{t-k}). This indicates whether price changes at time t are influenced by price changes occurring at k periods earlier.

For the time series ($x_1, x_2, x_3 .... x_t$), x_{t-1} - - - - - n terms the mean value is defined as

$$\bar{x} = \sum x_i / n$$

The sample standard deviation is

$$s_x = \sqrt{\frac{\sum (x_i - \bar{x})^2}{n-1}}$$

The population autocorrelation coefficient is estimated using the sample autocorrelation coefficient. The autocorrelation coefficient must be zero if the population is completely independent. Hence, the variation of sample autocorrelation coefficient from zero is a significant test for dependence or independence of random variables in a series. The log price of the first differences of time series is used to compute the autocorrelation. If no significant autocorrelations are found in the series, then the series is considered random.

The autocorrelation function ACF(k) for the time series Y_t and the k–lagged series Y_{t-k} is defined as:

$$ACF(k) = \frac{\sum_{t=k+1}^{n} (Y_t - \bar{Y})(Y_{t-k} - \bar{Y})}{\sum_{t=1}^{n} (Y_t - \bar{Y})^2}$$

Where $\bar{Y}$ is the overall mean of the series with n observations.

The standard error of ACF (k) is given by:

^{Se}ACF (k) = $1/\sqrt{n-k}$

When n is sufficiently large (n > 50), the approximate value of the standard error of ACF(k) is given by[15] :

$$^{Se}ACF(k) = \sqrt{\frac{1 + 2\sum_{i=1}^{k-1} r_i^2}{n}}$$

where

r_i = Autocorrelation at lag i

k = The time lag

n = Number of observations in the data series

To test whether ACF (k) are significantly different from zero, the following distribution of t is used:

$t = ACF(k) / Se_{ACF(k)}$

4.3.2 Ljung–Box Statistic

Ljung–Box (LB) statistic is used to test the joint hypothesis that all the autocorrelations for lag one through m are simultaneously equal to zero. The value of the LB statistic is compared with the chi-square table to assess if it is significant.

Ljung–Box statistic, is defined as

$$LB = n(n+2)\sum_{k=1}^{m}\left(\frac{r_k^{\,2}}{n-k}\right) \approx \chi^2 m$$

Where

n = The number of observations in the time series

k = The time lag

m= The number of time lags to be tested

r_k = Autocorrelation coefficients lagged at k time periods.

The LB statistic follows the chi-square distribution with m (the number of time lags to be tested) degrees of freedom. The null hypothesis is that all r_k are zero. If the computed LB exceeds the critical LB value from the chi-square table at the

Table 4.3: Autocorrelation and Ljung Box Tests for Daily Returns (China, Indonesia and Kola Lumpur) 2000–2012

Lag	*China*		*Indonesia*		*Kola Lumpur*	
	ACF	*Ljung Box*	*ACF*	*Ljung Box*	*ACF*	*Ljung Box*
1	0.002	0.013	0.129*	39.438*	–0.109*	35.477*
2	–0.016	0.787	0.027	41.136*	0.009	35.735*
3	0.035	4.282	0.013	41.547*	0.007	35.883*
4	0.039	8.748	0.003	41.574*	0.004	35.937*
5	–0.009	8.988	–0.022	42.669*	0.010	36.233*
6	–0.021	10.272	–0.008	42.804*	0.004	36.272*
7	0.025	12.082	–0.026	44.449*	0.013	36.743*
8	–0.027	14.177	–0.011	44.716*	0.015	37.417*
9	0.001	14.181	–0.026	46.271*	–0.003	37.443*
10	0.018	15.124	0.007	46.403*	0.014	38.003*
11	0.019	16.144	0.029	48.357*	0.016	38.475*
12	0.048*	22.929	0.023	49.559*	0.001	38.746*
13	0.031	25.738*	0.070*	61.131*	–0.039	43.368*
14	0.017	26.599*	0.066*	71.371*	0.007	43.515*
15	0.030	29.181*	–0.011	71.667*	–0.014	44.059*

* Significant at 5 per cent level.

Table 4.4: Autocorrelation and Ljung Box Tests for Daily Returns (Korea, India and Taiwan) 2000–2012

Lag	*Korea*		*India*		*Taiwan*	
	ACF	*Ljung Box*	*ACF*	*Ljung Box*	*ACF*	*Ljung Box*
1	0.015	0.577	0.083*	20.703	0.048*	7.456
2	–0.023	2.045	–0.043*	26.325	0.028	9.960
3	0.003	2.074	–0.013	26.821*	0.012	10.393
4	–0.010	2.326	0.014	27.415*	–0.047*	17.515
5	–0.051*	9.517	–0.012	27.850*	–0.009	17.798
6	0.030	11.913	–0.048*	34.727*	–0.042*	23.473
7	–0.033	14.845	0.009	34.972*	0.010	23.768*
8	0.015	15.470	0.049*	42.273*	0.015	24.497*
9	–0.012	15.882	0.025	44.083*	–0.018	25.487*
10	0.000	15.882	0.021	45.370*	0.016	26.348*
11	0.000	15.883	–0.019	46.419*	0.023	28.113*
12	–0.028	17.955	–0.012	46.867*	0.041	33.409*
13	0.031	20.653	0.026	48.931*	0.037	37.71*
14	–0.004	20.704	0.051*	56.701*	0.033	41.189*
15	–0.029	22.953	0.004	56.749*	–0.010	41.516*

* Significant at 5 per cent level.

Table 4.5: Autocorrelation and Ljung Box Tests for Daily Returns (Singapore, Australia and Japan) 2000–2012

Lag	*Singapore*		*Australia*		*Japan*	
	ACF	*Ljung Box*	*ACF*	*Ljung Box*	*ACF*	*Ljung Box*
1	0.010	0.312	–0.039	3.719	–0.030	2.619
2	0.035	4.073	0.012	4.077	–0.019	3.702
3	0.013	4.884	–0.041	8.221	–0.012	4.120
4	0.013	5.357	0.040	12.090	–0.022	5.587
5	0.021	6.688	0.029	14.166	–0.029	8.131
6	–0.044*	12.578	–0.024	15.587	0.006	8.221
7	0.019	13.698	–0.054*	22.758	0.018	9.136
8	–0.006	13.823	0.022	23.966*	–0.009	9.398
9	0.002	13.832	0.012	24.352*	–0.037	13.408
10	0.018	14.779	0.000	24.352*	0.031	16.317
11	–0.053*	23.383	–0.005	24.409*	0.021	17.636
12	0.034	26.972*	–0.025	25.907*	0.013	18.124
13	0.005	27.047*	0.036	29.080*	–0.004	18.167
14	0.011	27.386*	–0.015	29.647*	0.013	18.648
15	0.000	27.386*	–0.001	29.648*	0.017	19.487

* Significant at 5 per cent level.

Table 4.6: Autocorrelation and Ljung Box Tests for Daily Returns (France, Germany, Hong Kong UK and US) 2000–2012

Lag	*France*		*Germany*		*Hong Kong*		*UK*		*US*	
	ACF	*Ljung Box*	*ACF*	*Ljung Box*	*ACF*	*Ljung Box*	*ACF*	*Ljung Box*	*ACF*	*Ljung Box*
1	–0.034	3.474	–0.019	1.130	–0.027	2.233	–0.049*	7.202	–0.019	1.130
2	–0.043*	9.128	–0.015	1.848	0.003	2.258	–0.044*	13.122	–0.015	1.848
3	–0.066*	22.608	–0.036	5.778	–0.013	2.729	–0.086*	35.780*	–0.036	5.778
4	0.042*	27.995*	0.048*	12.888	–0.008	2.904	0.085*	57.666*	0.048*	12.888
5	–0.061*	39.359*	–0.049*	20.291	–0.040*	7.758	–0.057*	67.412*	–0.049*	20.291
6	–0.036	43.451*	–0.029	22.875	0.014	8.330	–0.046*	73.888*	–0.029	22.875
7	0.020	44.665*	0.004*	22.922	0.024	10.068	0.020	75.410*	0.004	22.922
8	0.045*	50.996*	0.040	27.714*	0.009	10.297	0.051*	83.134*	0.040*	27.714*
9	–0.048*	58.010*	–0.020	28.901*	–0.027	12.542	–0.011	83.471*	–0.020	28.901*
10	–0.026	60.089*	–0.015	29.573*	–0.049*	19.865	–0.020	84.663*	–0.015	29.573*
11	0.012	60.514*	–0.021	30.877*	0.009	20.098	–0.020	85.885*	0.021	30.877*
12	0.013	61.003*	0.017	31.785*	0.003	20.120	–0.001	85.886*	0.017	31.875*
13	0.013	61.824*	–0.004	31.544*	0.056*	29.572*	0.010	86.222*	–0.004	31.844*
14	0.013	62.328*	0.007	32.000*	–0.042*	34.779*	–0.018	87.189*	0.007	32.000*
15	0.013	62.826*	–0.016	32.764*	0.035	38.376*	0.018	88.163*	–0.016	32.764*

* Significant at 5 per cent level.

chosen level of significance, the null hypothesis is rejected. In such a situation, the result suggests dependency of the series, which violates the assumption of market efficiency. The chi-square value for fourteen degrees of freedom at 5 per cent level of significance is 23.6848. The results of the autocorrelation and Ljung–Box statistics, Dickey–Fuller test (Unit Root) and Augmented Dickey Fuller test are given in Table 4.3 to 4.14.

Table 4.7: Autocorrelation and Ljung Box Tests for Daily Returns (China, Indonesia and Kola Lumpur) 2000–2007

Lag	*China*		*Indonesia*		*Kola Lumpur*	
	ACF	*Ljung Box*	*ACF*	*Ljung Box*	*ACF*	*Ljung Box*
1	0.007	0.091	0.110*	20.982	0.201*	72.342*
2	–0.018	0.672	–0.006	21.038	0.022	73.223**
3	0.022	1.516	0.030	22.650	0.011	73.436*
4	0.036	3.763	0.009	22.791	–0.016	73.921*
5	–0.003	3.778	0.029	24.297*	–0.008	74.045*
6	–0.023	4.694	–0.002	24.302*	0.033	75.941*
7	0.027	6.003	–0.026	25.484*	0.025	77.081*
8	–0.020	6.697	–0.007	25.568*	0.018	77.633*
9	–0.008	6.818	0.002	25.578*	0.016	78.066*
10	0.013	7.111	0.023	26.524*	0.058*	84.111*
11	0.045*	10.634	0.065*	34.026*	0.016	84.558*
12	0.045*	14.209	–0.010	34.196*	–0.046*	88.307*
13	–0.005	14.254	–0.005	34.244*	–0.084*	100.961*
14	0.071*	23.165	0.027	35.492*	–0.028	102.418*
15	0.002	23.172	0.002	35.496*	0.003	102.438*

* Significant at 5 per cent level.

The auto-correlation coefficients for the log of the market return series for the whole study period show significant auto-correlation at different lags for the sample period. The results of Autocorrelation analysis and Ljung–Box statistics are given in Tables 4.3 to 4.6. It is performed for 15 lags of daily returns. In China the autocorrelation coefficient of, lag 12 is significant, for Indonesia autocorrelation coefficient of lag 1 lag13 and lag 14 are significant. For Kola Lumpur lag1 of daily return of autocorrelation coefficients are significant, in Korea 5th lag of daily return is 1st, 4th and 16th lags of daily return of Taiwan are significant. In Singapore lag 6, and lag11 are significant. Lag 7 is significant for Australia. For Japan all the logs are insignificant. Lag, 2, 3, 4, 5 and lag 8 lag 9 are significant for France. Lags 4 to lag 5and lag 7 are significant for Germany. For Hong –Kong lag 5 lag 10 and lag 13 are significant. Lags 1 to lag 6 and lag 8 are significant for UK. For US lag 4 and 5 and lag 8 are significant. The presence of non-zero auto-correlation coefficients in the log of the market returns series clearly suggest that there is a serial dependence between the values. The Ljung–Box statistics values are also provide the same results. Except

Table 4.8: Autocorrelation and Ljung Box Tests for Daily Returns (Korea, India and Taiwan) 2000–2007

Lag	*Korea*		*India*		*Taiwan*	
	ACF	*Ljung Box*	*ACF*	*Ljung Box*	*ACF*	*Ljung Box*
1	0.019	0.645	0.111*	22.445	0.037	2.436
2	–0.036	2.976	–0.083*	34.954*	0.033	4.326
3	–0.001	2.980	–0.011	35.158*	0.039	7.003
4	–0.006	3.052	0.059*	41.537**	–0.061*	13.697
5	–0.047	7.041	0.028	42.947*	0.009	13.854
6	0.018	7.619	–0.040	45.806*	–0.028	15.229
7	–0.026	8.877	–0.023	46.756*	–0.003	15.250
8	0.032	10.785	0.013	47.047*	–0.006	15.305
9	–0.030	12.401	0.037	49.562*	–0.016	15.772
10	–0.007	12.496	0.046*	53.384*	0.023	16.747
11	0.021	13.317	–0.022	54.254*	0.020	17.473
12	–0.025	14.488	–0.042	57.511*	0.072*	26.792*
13	0.014	14.863	0.025	58.699*	0.004	26.819*
14	0.001	14.865	0.044	62.226*	0.001	26.822*
15	–0.027	16.188	–0.033	62.243*	0.001	26.826*

* Significant at 5 per cent level.

Table 4.9: Autocorrelation and Ljung Box Tests for Daily Returns (Singapore, Australia and Japan) 2000–2007

Lag	*Singapore*		*Australia*		*Japan*	
	ACF	*Ljung Box*	*ACF*	*Ljung Box*	*ACF*	*Ljung Box*
1	0.029	1.559	–0.058*	6.089	–0.016	0.480
2	0.005	1.608	0.006	6.148	–0.015	0.879
3	0.065*	9.258	0.063*	13.467	0.014	1.207
4	0.045*	12.940	–0.008	13.589	–0.044*	4.615
5	0.018	13.520	–0.037	16.175	0.003	4.627
6	–0.073*	23.399	–0.028	17.601	–0.003	4.643
7	–0.006	23.454	–0.018	18.218	0.017	5.157
8	–0.003	23.485	0.035	20.464	–0.034	7.217
9	–0.026	24.684*	–0.030	22.088	–0.031	8.917
10	–0.019	25.370*	0.017	22.596	–0.021	9.723
11	0.020	26.127*	–0.005	22.647	0.012	9.988
12	0.005	26.181*	0.024	23.714*	–0.007	10.077
13	–0.012	26.445*	0.003	23.728*	0.000	10.077
14	–0.048*	30.617*	–0.036	26.118*	0.020	10.801
15	–0.018	31.186*	0.028	27.552*	–0.010	10.974

* Significant at 5 per cent level.

Table 4.10: Autocorrelation and Ljung Box Tests for Daily Returns (France, Germany, Hong Kong UK and US) 2000–2007

Lag	France		Germany		Hong Kong		UK		US	
	ACF	Ljung Box	ACF	Ljung Box	ACF	Ljung Box	ACF	Ljung Box	ACF	Ljung Box
1	–0.025	1.128	–0.037	2.583	0.004	0.035	–0.054*	5.277	–0.047*	4.073
2	–0.026	2.593	0.009	2.720	–0.020	0.752	–0.022	6.139	–0.086*	17.510
3	–0.050*	7.161	–0.019	3.421	0.058*	6.875	–0.088*	20.397	0.000	17.510
4	0.000	7.162	0.038	6.052	0.019	7.491	0.048*	24.679*	0.019	18.166
5	–0.061*	13.951	–0.055*	11.740	–0.059*	13.703	–0.030	26.350*	–0.046*	22.087
6	–0.064*	21.543	–0.057*	17.833	0.013	14.001	–0.050*	30.963*	0.000	22.087
7	0.017	22.190	0.011	18.053	0.027	15.341	0.012	31.229*	0.032	23.960*
8	0.063*	29.521*	0.077*	29.072*	–0.056*	20.984	0.053*	36.476*	–0.068*	32.447*
9	–0.012	29.798*	0.011	29.075*	0.000	20.984	0.029	38.035*	0.006	32.505*
10	–0.036	32.152*	0.059*	35.556*	0.005	21.025	–0.065*	45.909*	–0.009	32.670*
11	0.015	32.597*	0.013	35.850*	0.026	22.261	–0.032	47.814*	–0.027	33.977*
12	–0.020	33.314*	0.031	37.665*	–0.030	23.926*	–0.019	48.500*	–0.057*	39.870*
13	0.049	37.876*	–0.005	37.707*	0.031	25.668*	0.053*	53.737*	0.112*	62.948*
14	0.023	38.660*	0.019	38.410*	0.011	25.892*	–0.037	56.234*	–0.051*	67.640*
15	0.060*	45.662*	–0.001	38.466*	–0.002	25.896*	0.075*	66.680*	–0.030	69.248*

* Significant at 5 per cent level.

Korea and Japan the computed Ljung Box statistics for all the series at 15 lags are greater than the critical value of 23.68. Consequently the hypothesis of independence is rejected at a 5 per cent level of significance. Both autocorrelation and Ljung–Box tests prove that the market is not efficient at weak form for the whole study period.

Table 4.11: Autocorrelation and Ljung Box Tests for Daily Returns (China, Indonesia, Kola Lumpur, Korea and India) 2007–2012

Lag	*China*		*Indonesia*		*Kola Lumpur*	
	ACF	*Ljung Box*	*ACF*	*Ljung Box*	*ACF*	*Ljung Box*
1	–0.004	0.019	0.112*	14.539	–0.280*	92.058*
2	–0.015	0.275	0.063*	19.218	0.002	92.064*
3	0.045	2.624	–0.053	22.472	0.005	92.099*
4	0.034	3.979	–0.029	23.431	0.016	92.400*
5	–0.018	4.343	–0.061*	27.816*	0.020	92.888*
6	–0.010	4.460	–0.031	28.970*	–0.012	93.057*
7	0.021	4.963	0.005	28.996*	0.006	93.100*
8	–0.044	7.254	–0.010	29.104*	0.013	93.308*
9	0.010	7.363	–0.0310	30.172*	–0.014	93.533*
10	0.028	8.257	–0.007	30.237*	–0.011	93.680*
11	–0.011	8.388	–0.006	30.286**	0.016	93.970*
12	0.052	11.572	0.054	33.745*	0.026	94.768*
13	0.068*	17.037	0.112*	48.485*	–0.015	95.020*
14	–0.035	18.506	0.084*	56.805*	0.027	95.861*
15	0.054	21.890	0.007	56.863*	–0.023	96.496*

* Significant at 5 per cent level.

The auto-correlation coefficients for the log of the market return series before the Global crisis show significant auto-correlation at different lags for the sample period. The results of Autocorrelation analysis and Ljung–Box statistics are given in Tables 4.7 to 4.10. It is performed for 15 lags of daily returns. In China the autocorrelation coefficient of, lag 11, lag 12 and lag 14 are significant, for Indonesia autocorrelation coefficient of lag 1 and lag 11 are significant. For Kola Lumpur lag1 lag 10 lag12 and lag 13 of daily return of autocorrelation coefficients are significant, in Korea all the lags of daily return are insignificant. In India lag 1, lag 2, lag 4 and lag 10 are siginigicant 4th and 12th lags of daily return of Taiwan are significant. In Singapore lag3, lag 4, lag 6, and lag14 are significant. Lag 1 and lag 3 is significant for Australia. For Japan lag 4 is significant. Lag, 5,6 and lag 8 lag 15 are significant for France. Lags 5 to lag 6 and lag 8 and lag 10 are significant for Germany. For Hong –Kong lag 3 lag 5 and lag 8 are significant. Lags 1, to lag 6 and lag 8, lag 10, lag13 and lag 15 are significant for UK. For US lag 1, lag 2, lag5, lag 8 and lag 12, lag13 and lag 14 are significant. The presence of non-zero auto-correlation coefficients in the log of the market returns series before the global financial crisis clearly suggest that

Table 4.12: Autocorrelation and Ljung Box Tests for Daily Returns (Korea, India and Taiwan) 2007–2012

Lag	*Korea*		*India*		*Taiwan*	
	ACF	*Ljung Box*	*ACF*	*Ljung Box*	*ACF*	*Ljung Box*
1	0.014	0.214	0.056	3.724	0.064*	5.870
2	–0.005	0.243	0.006	3.766	0.021	6.506
3	–0.008	0.318	–0.015	4.048	–0.027	7.566
4	–0.037	1.875	–0.029	5.047	–0.027	8.607
5	–0.036	3.354	–0.051	8.075	–0.037	10524
6	0.021	3.869	–0.056	11.830	–0.062*	16.095
7	–0.013	4.076	0.039	13.668	0.028	17.200
8	–0.003	4.084	0.084*	22.071	0.044	19.912
9	0.011	4.224	0.012	22.236	–0.020	20498
10	–0.009	4.309	–0.004	22.257	0.004	20.526
11	–0.028	5.250	–0.016	22.551	0.026	21.504
12	0.009	5.336	0.016	22.860	–0.005	21.544
13	0.018	5.733	0.026	23.648*	0.081*	30.975*
14	–0.043	7.945	0.057	27.531*	0.076*	39.299*
15	–0.010	8.066	0.011	27.670*	–0.027	40.315*

* Significant at 5 per cent level.

Talbe 4.13: Autocorrelation and Ljung Box Tests for Daily Returns (Singapore, Australia and Japan) 2007–2012

Lag	*Singapore*		*Australia*		*Japan*	
	ACF	*Ljung Box*	*ACF*	*Ljung Box*	*ACF*	*Ljung Box*
1	–0.006	0.038	–0.013	0.237	–0.041	1.992
2	0.059	4.196	0.004	0.258	–0.023	2.610
3	–0.023	4.830	–0.062*	5.941	–0.034	3.921
4	–0.014	5.023	0.040	8.275	–0.005	3.948
5	0.023	5.701	0.010	8.418	–0.056	7.661
6	–0.021	6.256	–0.015	8.726	0.012	7.838
7	0.038	8.026	–0.051	12.507	0.018	8.204
8	–0.009	8.122	–0.020	13.076	0.011	8.353
9	0.024	8.835	0..028	14.248	–0.042	10.427
10	0.047	11.490	0.014	14.549	0.039	12.200
11	–0.113*	26.986*	–0.020	15.139	0.028	13.123
12	0.057	30.988*	–0.030	16.438	0.030	14.154
13	0.019	31.415*	0.036	18.345	–0.008	14.224
14	0.058	35.451*	0.002	18.353	0.006	14.267
15	0.013	35.651*	–0.011	18.527	0.039	16.073

* Significant at 5 per cent level.

Table 4.14: Autocorrelation and Ljung Box Tests for Daily Returns (France, Germany, Hong Kong UK and US) 2007–2012

Lag	*France*		*Germany*		*Hong Kong*		*UK*		*US*	
	ACF	*Ljung Box*	*ACF*	*Ljung Box*	*ACF*	*Ljung Box*	*ACF*	*Ljung Box*	*ACF*	*Ljung Box*
1	–0.042	2.138	0.004	0.016	–0.044	2.359	–0.045	2.438	–0.498*	297.603*
2	–0.056	6.027	–0.045	2.488	0.015	2.625	–0.061*	6.907	–0.001	297.605*
3	–0.082*	14.201	–0.057	6.448	–0.051	5.766	–0.085*	15.717	0.000	297.605*
4	0.079*	21.751	0.061*	11.061	–0.022	6.350	0.112*	30.895*	–0.002	297.610*
5	–0.061*	26.356*	–0.041	13.094	–0.030	7.450	–0.076*	37.887*	0.005	297.639*
6	–0.012	26.542*	0.005	13.128	0.015	7.705	–0.044	40.204*	–0.002	297.644*
7	0.022	27.137*	–0.005	13.158	0.021	8.262	0.027	41.056*	0.000	297.644*
8	0.030	28.278*	–0.005	13.190	0.044	10.550	0.051	44.156*	0.001	297.646*
9	–0.080*	36.127*	–0.043	15.465	–0.042	12.693	–0.040	46.130*	–0.001	297.647*
10	–0.019	36.551*	0.038	17.248	–0.080*	20.487	0.013	46.350*	–0.003	297.657*
11	0.009	36.647*	0.031	18.437	–0.001	20.488	–0.010	46.478*	0.001	297.660*
12	0.041	38.720*	0.000	18.437	0.019	20.943	0.013	46.682*	0.005	297.687*
13	–0.013	38.943*	–0.004	18.458	0.069*	26.759*	–0.022	47.251*	–0.003	297.697*
14	0.003	38.957*	–0.008	18.531	–0.071*	32.945*	–0.004	47.268*	–0.002	297.702*
15	–0.029	40.019*	–0.027	19.461	0.053	36.309*	–0.025	48.017*	–0.001	297.703*

* Significant at 5 per cent level.

there is a serial dependence between the values. The Ljung–Box statistics values are also provide the same results. Except Korea and Japan the computed Ljung Box statistics for all the series at 15 lags are greater than the critical value of 23.68. Consequently the hypothesis of independence is rejected at a 5 per cent level of significance. Both autocorrelation and Ljung–Box tests prove that the market is not efficient at weak form.

The auto-correlation coefficients for the log of the market return series after the Global crisis show significant auto-correlation at different lags for the sample period. The results of Autocorrelation analysis and Ljung–Box statistics are given in Tables 4.11 to 4.14. It is performed for 15 lags of daily returns. In China the autocorrelation coefficient of, lag 13 is significant, for Indonesia autocorrelation coefficient of lag 1, lag 2, lag 5, lag 13 and lag 14 are significant. For Kola Lumpur lag1 of daily return of autocorrelation coefficients is significant, in Korea all the lags of daily return are insignificant. In India lag 8 is significant lag 1, lag 6, lag 13 and lag14 of daily return of Taiwan are significant. In Singapore lag11 is significant. In Australia and Japan all the lags are insignificant. Lags 3 to lag 5 and lag 9 are significant for France. Only lag 4 is significant for Germany. For Hong –Kong lag 10 lag 13 and lag 14 are significant. Lag 2 to lag 5 is significant for UK. For US lag 1, is significant. The presence of non-zero auto-correlation coefficients in the log of the market returns series after the global financial crisis clearly suggest that there is a serial dependence between the values. The Ljung–Box statistics values are also provide the same results. Except Korea and Japan the computed Ljung Box statistics for all the series at 15 lags are greater than the critical value of 23.68. Consequently the hypothesis of independence is rejected at a 5 per cent level of significance. Both autocorrelation and Ljung–Box tests prove that the market is not efficient at weak form.

4.3.4 Augmented Dickey–Fuller Test (Unit Root) and Philip Peron Test

The Dickey–Fuller statistic applies only to an autoregression (1) model. For some series autoregression (1) model does not capture all the serial correlation in (y_t). In Dickey–Fuller test it is assumed that the white noise error term is uncorrelated. Dickey and Fuller have developed a higher order autoregression, the Augmented Dickey–Fuller (ADF) test, in case μ_t are correlated. They have augmented the Dickey Fuller test by including the lagged value of the dependent variable ΔY_t, the result is known as Augmented Dickey–Fuller Test (Unit Root)

The Augmented Dickey–Fuller (ADF) test is estimated by the following formula:

$$\Delta Y_t = \beta_1 + \beta_2 t + \delta Y_{t-1} + \alpha_i \sum_{i=1}^{m} \Delta Y_{t-i} + \mu_t$$

Where μ_t is a white noise error term and $\Delta Y_{t-1} = (Y_{t-1} - Y_{t-2})$. The null hypothesis $H_0: \delta = 0$, and the alternative hypothesis $H_1: \delta < 0$.The critical value of ADF test at 5 per cent level of significance is –3.41.

Table 4.15: Augmented Dickey–Fuller Test on Market Index Levels (2000–2012)

Name of the Indices	*Augmented Dickey - Fuller Test*			*Phillip Peron Test*	
	β_1	β_2	δ	*T- Stat*	*P- Value*
China	0.009 (1.341)	0.000 (0.225)	–0.001 (–1.280)	–1.377	0.595
Indonesia	0.019 (2.492)	0.000 (2.668)	–0.003 (–2.496)	–2.517	0.319
Kola Lumpur	0.034 (3.319)	0.000 (3.657)	–0.005 (–3.356)	–1.702	0.750
Korea	0.038 (3.156)	0.000 (3.238)	–0.006 (–3.175)	–3.137	0.097
India	0.020 (2.323)	0.000 (2.226)	–0.002 (–2.298)	–2.364	0.398
Taiwan	0.049 (3.737)	0.000 (3.044)	–0.005 (–3.789)	–3.812	0.016
Australia	0.014 (1.484)	0.000 (0.998)	–0.001 (–1.465)	–1.043	0.739
Singapore	0.018 (2.075)	0.000 (1.882)	–0.002 (–2.088)	–2.176	0.502
Japan	0.029 (2.398)	0.000 (0.161)	–0.003 (–2.456)	–2.354	0.403
France	0.018 (1.679)	0.000 (–0.317)	–0.002 (–1.715)	–2.002	0.286
Germany	0.022 (2.289)	0.000 (1.736)	–0.002 (–2.349)	–2.341	0.410
Hong Kong	0.035 (2.629)	0.000 (2.343)	–0.003 (–2.650)	–2.594	0.282
US	0.028 (2.938)	0.000 (2.688)	–0.004 (–3.118)	–3.072	0.113
UK	0.029 (2.251)	0.000 (1.305)	–0.003 (–2.287)	–2.552	0.302

Figures in the parentheses are tau (τ) values * Significant at 1 per cent level.

The critical values for the ADF test statistics are -3.413 and -3.964 at the 5 per cent and 1 per cent levels, respectively.

PP critical values are: -3.435, -2.863 and -2.567 at 1 per cent, 5 per cent and 10 per cent respectively.

Table 4.16: Augmented Dickey–Fuller Test on Market Index Levels (2000–2007)

Name of the Indices	Augmented Dickey - Fuller Test			Phillip Peron Test	
	β_1	β_2	δ	T- Stat	P- Value
China	–0.010 (–1.034)	0.000 (1.937)	0.001 (0.978)	0.970	0.999
Indonesia	0.026 (2.827)	0.000 (2.827)	–0.004 (–2.899)	–2.951	0.146
Kola Lumpur	0.030 (2.818)	0.000 (3.861)	–0.004 (–2.890)	–2.894	0.164
Korea	0.050 (3.030)	0.000 (3.574)	–0.008 (–3.086)	–3.020	0.126
India	0.021 (2.121)	0.000 (2.937)	–0.003 (–2.192)	–2.431	0.362
Taiwan	0.058 (3.263)	0.000 (3.537)	–0.006 (–3.358)	–2.431	0.362
Australia	0.012 (1.125)	0.000 (2.070)	–0.001 (–1.145)	–1.097	0.927
Singapore	0.014 (1.382)	0.000 (2.784)	–0.002 (–1.459)	–1.482	0.835
Japan	0.033 (2.443)	0.000 (2.443)	–0.003 (–2.560)	–2.560	0.299
France	0.012 (1.113)	0.00 (1.870)	–0.001 (–1.210)	–0.973	0.945
Germany	0.010 (0.933)	0.00 (2.451)	–0.001 (–1.072)	–0.970	0.946
Hong Kong	0.023 (1.693)	0.000 (2.917)	–0.002 (–1.771)	–1.781	0.713
US	0.025 (2.068)	0.000 (1.670)	–0.003 (–2.282)	–2.294	0.436
UK	0.016 (1.215)	0.000 (2.192)	–0.001 (–1.285)	–1.252	0.8983

Figures in the parentheses are tau (τ) values * Significant at 1 per cent level.

The critical values for the ADF test statistics are -3.413 and -3.964 at the 5 per cent and 1 per cent levels, respectively.

PP critical values are: -3.435, -2.863 and -2.567 at 1 per cent, 5 per cent and 10 per cent respectively.

Table 4.17: Augmented Dickey–Fuller Test (2007–2012)

Name of the Indices	*Augmented Dickey - Fuller Test*			*Phillip Peron Test*	
	β_1	β_2	δ	*T- Stat*	*P- Value*
China	0.030 (1.445)	0.000 (–0.740)	–0.003 (–1.471)	–1.495	0.141
Indonesia	0.025 (1.543)	0.000 (1.597)	–0.003 (–1.555)	–1.446	0.847
Kola Lumpur	0.032 (1.629)	0.000 (1.629)	–0.004 (–1.674)	–1.702	0.750
Korea	0.047 (2.059)	0.000 (1.647)	–0.006 (–2.089)	–2.069	0.705
India	0.041 (1.718)	0.000 (0.632)	–0.004 (1.713)	–1.798	0.086
Taiwan	0.035 (1.779)	0.000 (0.923)	–0.004 (–1.810)	–1.831	0.689
Australia	0.042 (2.014)	0.000 (–0.027)	–0.005 (–2.049)	–1.975	0.611
Singapore	0.027 (1.599)	0.000 (1.216)	–0.003 (–1.657)	–1.655	0.097
Japan	0.075 (2.234)	0.000 (–0.600)	–0.008 (–2.287)	–2.119	0.533
France	0.065 (2.278)	0.000 (–0.710)	–0.007 (–2.324)	–1.956	0.623
Germany	0.050 (1.979)	0.000 (1.053)	–0.005 (–2.022)	–2.022	0.043
Hong Kong	0.063 (1.945)	0.000 (–0.027)	–0.006 (–1.952)	–1.831	0.688
US	0.032 (1.556)	0.000 (1.895)	–0.004 (–1.597)	–1.563	0.806
UK	0.064 (2.250)	0.000 (0.925)	–0.007 (–2.280)	–2.064	0.564

Figures in the parentheses are tau (τ) values * Significant at 1 per cent level.

The critical values for the ADF test statistics are -3.413 and -3.964 at the 5 per cent and 1 per cent levels, respectively.

PP critical values are: -3.435, -2.863 and -2.567 at 1 per cent, 5 per cent and 10 per cent respectively.

The calculated τ (tau) values of δ in the Augmented Dickey Fuller test and Phillip Peron test for the whole period (2000–2012) are insignificant at 5 per cent level for all the countries. The empirical result summarizes that, the variables at level are non-stationary, therefore the stock prices are independent of the past stock price and the successive random error terms are also independent of the past errors.

The calculated τ (tau) values of δ in the Augmented Dickey Fuller test and Phillip Peron test for the pre-crisis period (2000–2007) are insignificant at 5 per cent level for all the countries. The empirical result summarizes that, the variables at level are non-stationary, therefore the stock prices are independent of the past stock price and the successive random error terms are also independent of the past errors

The calculated τ (tau) values of δ in the Augmented Dickey Fuller test and Phillip Peron test for the post-crisis period (2007–2012) are insignificant at 5 per cent level for all the countries. The empirical result summarises that, the variables at level are non-stationary, therefore the stock prices are independent of the past stock price and the successive random error terms are also independent of the past errors.

4.4 Conclusion

The behavior of stock prices in the developed and the emerging stock markets are analysed. The daily returns of stock price are examined. The traditional test namely Kolmogorov Smirnov Goodness of Fit Test (K-S test) runs test, autocorrelation test, Ljung Box test and the dynamic test the Augmented Dickey Fuller test and Philip Peron test are employed to examine the efficiency of the market. The hypothesis of the randomness of the stock returns are rejected for stock price index changes at all frequencies using Kolmogorov Smirnov Goodness of Fit Test (K-S test), Run Test auto correlation test and Ljung Box test. The rejection of null hypothesis indicates that the market is not weak form efficient. But the unit root hypothesis provides sufficient evidence that stock prices of all the stock markets follow random walk process. The results of the non-stationary variables support random walk hypothesis. On the basis of the unit root test (nonstationarity) it is confirmed that all stock markets are weak form efficient.

References

1. Poshakwale, S. (1996). Evidence on Weak Form Efficiency and Day of the Week Effect in the Indian Stock Market. **Finance India**, Vol X, No. 3. 605-616.
2. Fama, E. (1965), "The behavior of Stock Market Prices", **Journal of Business**, vol 38, p.34-105.
3. Fama, E. (1970). Efficient Capital Markets: A Review of Theory and Empirical Work, **Journal of Finance**, 25, 283-306.
4. Fama, E. (1991). Efficient Capital Markets II, **Journal of Finance**, 46, 1575-1671.
5. **ICIF**
6. Asma Mobarek Kevin Keasey, (2000) "Weak-Form Efficiency of an Emerging Market: Evidence from the Dhaka Stock Exchange of Bangladesh", The paper presented at the ENBS Conference held on OSLO May 2000. www.bath.ac.uk/cds/enbs-papers-pdfs/mobarek-new.pdf
7. Working, H., 1934, "A random-Difference Series for the use in the Analysis of Time series," 30 **Journal of the American Statistics Association**, (March) pp.11-22.
8. Kendall, M. G. (1943), **The advanced Theory of Statistics**, Vol.1, London: Griffin.

9. Kendall, M. G. (1953), "The analysis of Economic Time–series", Part1. Prices, **The Journal of the Royal statistical Society**,116,pp.11-25.

10. Cootner, P. (1962), "Stock Prices: Random vs. Systematic Changes", **Industrial Management Review,** vol. 3, spring, pp.24-45.

11. Osborne, M.F.M. (1962), "Periodic Structure In the Brownian Motion in the Stock Prices," **Operation Research**, (May/June),Pp.345-379.

12. Fama, E. (1965), **Op.Cit.,**

13. Groenewold, N. and Kang, K.C. (1993). The Semi-strong Efficiency of the Australian Share Market, **Economic Record**, Vol. 69, Iss. 207, December, 405-410.

14. Narayan and Russel Smyth, (2005) **"Cointegration of Stock Markets between New Zealand, Australia and the G7 Economies: Searching for Co-Movement under Structural Change", Australian Economic Papers, Vol.44, No.3, 2005, pp.231–247.**

15. Fama, Eugune F.,and Kenneth R.French, (1988), "Permanent and temporary components of stock market prices", **Journal of Political Economy**, vol. 96, pp-246-273.

16. Poterba, James M and Lawerence H. Summers, (1988), "Mean reversion of stock prices",**Journal of Financial Economics**, vol. 22, pp-27-59.

17. Hudson, Robert. Dempsey, Michael and Keasey, Kevin., "A note on the weak-form efficiency of capital markets: The application of simple technical trading rules to UK Stock prices-1935 to1994", **Journal of Banking and Finance**, vol.20, Pp. 1121-1132.

18. Kwan, A. A. Sim and J. Cotsomitis, "The Causal Relationships between Equity Indices on World Exchanges", **Applied Economics**, Vol.27, No.1, 1995, pp.33–37.

19. Nicolaas Groenewold, (1997), "Share market efficiency: Tests using daily data for Australia and New Zealand", **Applied Financial Economics**, vol.7. Pp.645-657.

20. Branes Paul, (1986), " Thin trading and stock market efficiency: A case of the Kuala Lumpur Stock Exchange", **Journal of Business Finance and Accounting**, volume 13(4) winter, pp. 609- 617.

21. Chan Kam C. Gup Benton E., and Pan Ming-shiun, (1992), "An Empirical Analysis of Stock Prices in Major Asian Markets and United States", **The financial Review**, vol-27, no-2, May1992, pp-289-307.

22. Dickinson and Muragu, (1994), " Market Efficiency in Developing Countries: A case study of the Nairobi Stock Exchange", **Journal of Business Finance and Accounting**, volume 21(1) January, pp. 133-150.

23. Ojah Kalu and Karemera,(1999), " Random walks and Market efficiency Tests of Latin Amaeracan Emerging Equity Markets: A Revisit", **The Financial Review,** volume 34, pp. 57-72.

24. Amanulla, S. and Hamaiah, "Indian Stock Market: Is it Informationally efficient?", **Prajnan,** Vol.26, No. 4, 1997–98, pp.473–479.

25. Ramasastri, A.S. (2000) "Market Efficiency in the Nineties: Testing through Unit Root", **Prajnan,** Vol. 28, No.2, 1999–2000, pp.155–162.

26. Pradhan, H.K and Lakshmi S. Narasimhan,(2002) "Stock Price Behaviour in India since Liberalization", **Asia-Pacific Development Journal**, Vol.9, No.2, 2002, pp.84–107.

27. Hasan, M. S. (2004), "On the Validity of the Random Walk Hypothesis Applied to the Dhaka Stock Exchange," **International Journal of Theoretical and Applied Finance**, Vol. 7, Iss 8; p. 106

28. Roux and Gilbertson, (1978), "The behavior of share prices on the Johannesburg StockExchange", **Journal of Business Finance and Accounting**, Volume5(2), pp. 223-232.

29. Claessens Stijin, Dasgupta Susmita, and Glen Jack, (1995); "Return behaviour in emerging Stock Market", **The world Bank economic Review**, vol.9, no.1, Pp. 131-151.

30. Poshakwale, S. (1996). **Op.Cit.,**

31. Nourredine Khababa, (1998), "Behavior of stock prices in the Saudi Arabian Financial Market: Empirical research findings", Journal of Financial Management and Analysis, Volume 11(1), Jan-June, pp. 48-55.

32. Madhusoodanan, T.P.,(1998) "Persistence in the Indian Stock Market Returns: An Application of Variance Ratio Test", **Vikalpa**, Vol.23, No.4, 1998, pp.61-73.

33. Asma Mobarek Kevin Keasey, (2000), **Op.Cit.,**

34. Hyun-Jung Ryoo, Graham Smith, (2000) "Korean Stock Prices under Price Limits: VarianceRatioTestsofRandomWalks".www.Soas.ac.uk/department/departmentinfo.cfm?navid=469. 2000.

35. Sarath, P. Abeysekera,(2001) "Efficient Markets Hypothesis and the Emerging Capital Market in Sri Lanka: Evidence from the Colombo Stock Exchange – A Note", **Journal of Business Finance and Accounting**, vol.28, No.1 and 2, 2001, pp.249–261.

36. Sunil Poshakwale, "The Random Walk Hypothesis in the Emerging Indian Stock Market", **Journal of Business Finance and Accounting,** Vol.29, No.9 and 10, 2002, pp.1275–1299.

37. Chaudhuri, K. and Wu, Y., 2003, "Random walk versus breaking trend in stock prices: Evidence from emerging markets," **Journal of Banking and Finance**, Vol. 27(4), pages 575-592

38. Ibrahim Awad and Zahran Daraghma (2009) "Testing the Weak-Form Efficiency of the Palestinian Securities Market" International Research Journal of Finance and EconomicsISSN 1450-2887 Issue 32 (2009) http://www.eurojournals.com/finance.htm

Chapter 5

Return and Volatility in Indian and International Stock Markets

5.1 Introduction

Financial markets play an important role in the process of economic growth and development by facilitating savings and channeling funds from savers to investors. Risks are omnipresent and exist from time immemorial. Uncertainty is the hallmark of the securities market. Volatility in financial markets has always been a key element in investment decisions and modeling financial markets. A fluctuation in price of broad stock market indexes over defined period is known as stock market volatility. Volatility is the parameter that enables the investor to compare the risk and reward associated with various stocks and other asset classes. This comparison helps to determine the portfolio diversification for an investor. Volatility may thwart the smooth functioning of the financial system and adversely affect economic performance. Volatility in stock market is the relative rate at which the price of a security moves up and down.

Volatility is often viewed as a negative term, in the market that portrays uncertainty and risk. There are many definitions of volatility but in simple words volatility is "the rate and magnitude of changes in price", it is about how fast prices move. Volatility is low when the market is smooth but moving in range of trade. The ups and downs of the financial markets are always common. Stock market volatility may also affect business investment (Zuliu, 1995) and economic growth directly (Levine and Zervos, 1996 and Arestis *et al.*, 2001). Higher volatility frustrates the investors as they watch the value of their portfolios move wildly and decrease in value. Volatility can influence investors to respond irrationally, selling when the price of the shares have fallen to a low. Speculators like day traders hope to make money through volatility.

Negative incidences or events such as country's depression or recession, political turmoil or instability or chaos that occur internally or externally enhance volatility and have negative impact on its performance. Global financial crisis is a major turmoil event which permeated all over the world irrespective of developed or emerging developing countries. Volatility is an important element in taking decisions regarding portfolio diversification and hedging plans. Sometimes, the investors are forced to quit the market because of persistent higher negative volatility due to negative shock.

This crisis originated in United States in second half of 2007 with subprime mortgage crisis and got worst momentum in the year 2008. The crisis affected the whole world rapidly due to technological advancement and globalization. Developing countries experienced adverse impact on their economies via the channel of finance and trade. FIIs investment from developed countries to developing countries tumbled down from the beginning of this crisis. This crisis badly affected FDI, portfolio investment and exports of the developing countries (Iqbal, 2010). Like other sectors, world's stock markets also affected by this storm and faced bear trend from the first month of 2008.

Existing studies of volatility across markets, (Bekaert and Harvey 1995), have shown that the characteristics of emerging market equities are vastly different from developed markets' equities. The emerging market returns in the past have demonstrated certain distinguishing features; average returns were higher, correlation with developed market returns was low, investors looked to emerging markets for risk diversification. This analysis helps to understand the time series variation and higher order moments in the volatility of equities in these markets.

For the Indian investors, regulators, brokers, policy makers, dealers and researchers the issues of return and volatility have become increasingly important with the increase in the foreign institutional investors investment. It is necessary to understand and assess volatility effectively, keeping in mind possible behavioral biases. Hence an attempt has been made to analyze volatility among various countries and at various phases.

5.2 Frame Work of Analysis

Volatility is the most important statistical measure. The market risk of a single instrument or an entire portfolio of instruments is measured by volatility. Statistically, volatility of a random variable is its standard deviation of the return. In day-to-day practice, volatility is calculated for all sorts of random financial variables such as stock return, interest rate, the market value of portfolio, etc. Stock return volatility measures the random variability of the stock returns. Simply put stock return volatility is the variation of the stock return in time. More specifically, it is the standard deviation of the daily stock return around the mean value and the stock market volatility is the return volatility of the aggregate market portfolio. Stock market volatility indicates the degree of price variation between the share prices during a particular period. A certain degree of market volatility is unavoidable, even desirable, as the stock price fluctuation indicates changing values across economic activities and it facilitates better resource allocation. But frequent and wide stock market variations cause uncertainty about the value of an asset and affect the confidence of the investors. The risk averse and the risk neutral investors may withdraw from a market at sharp price movements. Extreme volatility disrupts the smooth functioning of the stock market. The voluminous literature on stock market volatility stated that the overall stock market volatility has fluctuated over the time with no discernible trend and some authors have argued that volatility is higher during the bear markets. In this study, inter-day and intra-day volatility are calculated for each year.

5.2.1 Volatility

Average daily volatility of a stock or index is measured by calculating the standard deviation of logarithmic returns during a certain period. Standard deviation is used as a proxy for variability in stock prices. As a first step,

Return is calculated using logarithmic method as follows.

$$r_t = (\log p_t - \log p_{t-1})$$

where,

r_t = Market return at the period t

P_t = Price index at day t

P_{t-1} = Price index at day $_{t-1}$ and

log = Natural log

5.2.2 Skewness

Skewness is a measure of the asymmetry of the probability distribution of a real-valued random variable. Skewness is the standardized 3rd central moment of a distribution. Positive skewness indicates a long right tail. Negative skewness indicates a long left tail. Zero skewness indicates symmetry around the mean

Return series may not be normally distributed and often tend to exhibit excess kurtosis, so that extreme values are more likely than the normal distribution would suggest. Such fat tailed distributions are common with financial parameters. Skewness is also common, especially with equity returns, where big down moves are typically more likely than comparable, big up-moves.

If the returns are normally distributed, then coefficients of skewness should be equal to zero. The following model is used to measure non-normality or asymmetry of equity return.

$$Sk = (n^2 / (n-1)(n-2)(m_3 / s^3)$$

where,

n = Sample size,

m_3 = Third moment about the mean, and

s = Standard deviation

5.2.3 Excess Kurtosis

Kurtosis is the standardized 4th central moment of a distribution. The normal distribution is 3.Positive excess kurtosis indicates flatness (long, fat tails). Negative excess kurtosis indicates peakedness. Excess kurtosis is measured by the following model.

$$Ku = [n^2 / (n-1)(n-2)(n-3)]\{(n+1)m_4 - 3(n+1)m_2^2\} / s^4$$

where,

n = Sample size

m_4 = Fourth moment about the mean,

m_2 = Second moment about the mean, and

s = Standard deviation

5.2.4 Inter-day Volatility

The variation in share price return between the two trading days is called inter-day volatility. Inter-day volatility is computed by close to close and open to open value of any index level on a daily basis. Standard deviation is used to calculate inter-day volatility. The inter-day volatility is calculated by close to close and open to open volatility method.

5.2.5 Close to Close Volatility

For computing close to close volatility, the closing values of the S and P CNX Nifty, the CNX Nifty Junior, the CNX 200 and the S and P CNX 500 are taken. Close to close volatility (standard estimation of volatility) is measured with the following formula:

$$\sigma = \sqrt{(1/n-1)\sum(r_t - \bar{r})^2}$$

where,

n = The number of trading days

r_t = Close to close return (in natural log)

$\bar{r}$ = Average of the close to close return

5.2.6 Open to Open Volatility

Open to open volatility is considered necessary for many market participants because opening prices of shares and the index values reflect any positive or negative information that arrives after the close of the market and before the start of the next day's trading. The following formula is used to calculate open to open volatility:

$$\sigma = \sqrt{(1/n-1)\sum(r_t-\bar{r})^2}$$

where,

n = The number of trading days

r_t = Open to open return (in natural log)

$\bar{r}$ = Average of the close to close return

Inter-day volatility takes into account only close to close and open to open index value and it is measured by standard deviation of returns.

5.2.7 Intra-day Volatility

Stock prices change minute-by-minute even second by second and it affects the profitability of the brokers and the investors and it influences the market participants' decision. The variation in share price return within the trading day is called intra-day volatility. It indicates how the indices and shares behave in a particular day. Intra-day volatility is calculated with the help of Parkinson Model and Garman and Klass model.

5.2.8 Parkinson Model

High–low volatility is calculated with the following formula:

$$\sigma = k\sqrt{1/n\sum \log(H_t/L_t)^2}$$

where,

σ = High–Low volatility

k = 0.601

H_t = High price on the day

L_t = Low price on the day

n = Number of trading days

5.2.9 Garman and Klass Model

The Garman and Klass model is used to calculate the open–close volatility. The formula for Garman and Klass model (1980) takes the following form.

$$\sigma = \sqrt{1/n\sum(1/2)[\log(H_t/L_t)]^2 - [2\log(2)-1][\log(C_t/O_t)]^2}$$

where,

H_t = High price on the day

L_t = Low price on the day

C_t = Closing price on the day

O_t = Opening price on the day

n = Number of trading days

σ = Intra-day volatility for the period

5.3 Return

Return is the motivating factor that induces the investors to invest money in shares. Return means the profit earned as a result of rise in share prices. Return helps the investor to compare the benefits available in the alternative investment avenue. Descriptive statistics are used to analyze the return of the stock markets and the results are given in Tables 5.1–5.4.

Table 5.1: Stock Index Daily Average Return and Volatility (percentage) (Emerging Countries China, Indonesia and Kola Lumpur)

Year	*China*		*Indonesia*		*Kola Lumpur*	
	Mean	*Std*	*Mean*	*Std*	*Mean*	*Std*
2000-2001	0.0675	0.996	–0.1759	1.530	–0.1710	1.244
2001-2002	–0.1177	1.672	0.1095	1.349	0.0638	1.269
2002-2003	–0.0247	1.274	–0.1306	1.508	–0.0699	0.808
2003-2004	0.0590	1.129	0.2538	1.238	0.1421	0.734
2004-2005	–0.1597	1.310	0.1574	1.288	–0.0138	0.644
2005-2006	0.0443	1.475	0.0824	1.166	0.0249	0.465
2006-2007	0.3753	1.738	0.1320	1.344	0.1196	0.800
2007-2008	0.0358	2.395	0.1189	1.805	0.0002	1.251
2008-2009	–0.1553	2.752	–0.0181	2.304	–0.0974	1.135
2009-2010	0.1125	1.72	0.2708	1.440	0.1644	2.6153
2010-2011	–0.0247	1.416	0.1142	1.319	0.0635	0.563
2011-2012	–0.1056	1.193	0.0462	1.401	0.0133	0.693
2000–2007	0.056	1.488	0.0746	1.345	0.0185	0.891
2007-2012	–0.045	1.949	0.056	1.728	0.014	1.484
2000–2012	0.0163	1.686	0.0680	1.510	0.0170	1.164

Tables 5.1–5.4 provide details of daily mean return and daily standard deviations for the sample countries over 12 year period from 2000 to 2012. Daily mean return and volatility (standard deviation) are calculated for each country. However, in the long run (2006 - 2007) daily return works out to 0.3753 per cent for China. Emerging markets performed better than developed markets. China, Indonesia and India performed better than the rest of the emerging markets and many of the major markets. India, Hong-Kong and Japan suffered loss consecutively for three years from 2000-2001 to 2002-2003. In the year 2000 – 2001 except China all the market suffered loss and it was very high in US (–0.394). The global financial crisis affected all the stock markets in the year 2008-2009 and the loss was very high in Singapore (–0.2254). The market suffered loss in the year 2008-2009 due to global financial crisis. The end of 3rd quarter 2008 was characterized by huge

Table 5.2: Stock Index Daily Average Return and Volatility (percentage) (Emerging Countries Korea, India and Taiwan)

Year	*Korea*		*India*		*Taiwan*	
	Mean	*Std*	*Mean*	*Std*	*Mean*	*Std*
2000-2001	–0.211	2.866	–0.1139	1.984	–0.2201	2.374
2001-2002	0.2203	2.052	–0.0066	1.404	0.0256	1.917
2002-2003	–0.2081	2.060	–0.0573	0.992	–0.1428	1.773
2003-2004	0.2028	1.376	0.2338	1.433	0.1640	1.307
2004-2005	0.0329	1.488	0.0548	1.641	–0.0331	1.325
2005-2006	0.1358	1.106	0.2046	1.036	0.0388	0.859
2006-2007	0.0269	1.086	0.0466	1.776	0.0717	1.055
2007-2008	0.0654	1.629	0.0853	2.025	0.0344	1.585
2008-2009	–0.1393	2.554	–0.1848	2.664	–0.2015	2.095
2009-2010	0.1344	1.763	0.2264	1.882	0.1681	1.404
2010-2011	0.0885	0.944	0.0415	1.118	0.0366	0.989
2011-2012	–0.0180	1.642	–0.0393	1.301	–0.0551	1.352
2000–2007	0.0396	1.789	0.0571	1.498	–0.006	1.569
2007-2012	0.012	1.723	0.017	1.906	–0.008	1.471
2000–2012	0.0293	1.763	0.0413	1.670	–0.0079	1.567

Table 5.3: Stock Index Daily Average Return and Volatility (percentage) (Developed Countries Australia, Singapore and Japan)

Year	*Australia*		*Singapore*		*Japan*	
	Mean	*Std*	*Mean*	*Std*	*Mean*	*Std*
2000-2001	–0.0046	0.808	–0.0971	1.481	–0.1826	1.616
2001-2002	0.0330	0.783	0.0298	1.443	–0.0675	1.826
2002-2003	–0.0651	0.770	–0.1397	1.120	–0.1317	1.531
2003-2004	0.0715	0.468	0.1518	1.028	0.1551	1.368
2004-2005	0.0718	0.425	0.0557	0.718	–0.0016	1.057
2005-2006	0.0845	0.629	0.0661	0.598	0.1543	1.081
2006-2007	0.0638	0.848	0.0973	1.042	0.0053	1.147
2007-2008	–0.0396	1.402	–0.0300	1.587	–0.1320	1.565
2008-2009	–0.1658	1.942	–0.2254	2.204	–0.1774	2.936
2009-2010	0.1282	1.121	0.2061	1.325	0.1282	1.421
2010-2011	0.0028	0.929	0.0282	0.841	–0.0523	1.594
2011-2012	–0.0430	1.121	–0.0122	1.133	0.0135	1.141
2000–2007	0.037	0.696	0.029	1.099	–0.007	1.388
2007-2012	–0.024	1.327	–0.013	1.514	–0.050	1.880
2000–2012	0.0107	1.030	0.0123	1.280	–0.0244	1.600

Table 5.4: Stock Index Daily Average Return and Volatility (percentage) (Developed Countries France, Germany, Hong-Kong US and UK)

Year	*France*		*Germany*		*Hong-Kong*		*US*		*UK*	
	Mean	*Std*	*Mean*	*Std*	*Mean*	*Std*	*Mean*	*Std*	*Mean*	*Std*
2000-2001	–0.1047	1.442	–0.0767	1.424	–0.1267	1.801	–0.3938	3.878	–0.0592	1.164
2001-2002	–0.0308	1.754	–0.0397	1.576	–0.0607	1.704	–0.0103	2.917	–0.0265	1.225
2002-2003	–0.3151	2.783	–0.2275	2.450	–0.0984	1.167	–0.1546	2.683	–0.1493	1.921
2003-2004	0.1828	1.494	0.1270	1.165	0.1543	1.063	0.1388	1.387	0.0762	0.860
2004-2005	0.0470	0.886	0.0448	0.789	0.0259	0.962	0.0043	1.111	0.0437	0.598
2005-2006	0.1218	0.811	0.0959	0.724	0.0625	0.721	0.0592	0.864	0.0775	0.584
2006-2007	0.0579	0.996	0.0299	0.968	0.0898	1.043	0.0153	1.007	0.0222	0.843
2007-2008	–0.0228	1.316	–0.0713	1.390	0.0572	2.192	0.01804	1.410	–0.0403	1.375
2008-2009	–0.1835	2.454	–0.2011	2.587	–0.2074	3.056	–0.1608	2.806	–0.1463	2.399
2009-2010	0.1357	1.382	0.1600	1.422	0.1762	1.714	0.1823	1.182	0.1459	1.130
2010-2011	0.0014	1.463	0.0520	1.142	0.0402	1.080	0.0911	1.186	0.0156	1.107
2011-2012	–0.0592	1.809	–0.0052	1.851	–0.0540	1.613	0.0491	1.448	–0.0095	1.329
2000–2007	–0.002	1.395	0.0365	1.569	0.012	1.251	–0.041	2.221	0.001	1.102
2007-2012	–0.046	1.822	–0.000	0.017	–0.004	2.082	0.026	1.88	–0.011	1.579
2000–2012	–0.0189	1.578	–0.0035	1.639	0.0065	1.634	–0.0143	2.051	–0.0037	1.312

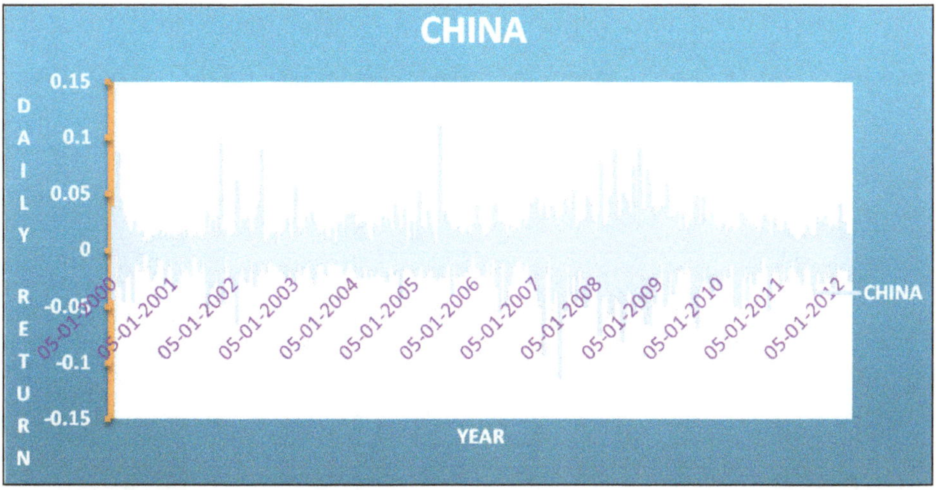

Figure 5.1: Stock Index Daily Average Return China (2000–2012).

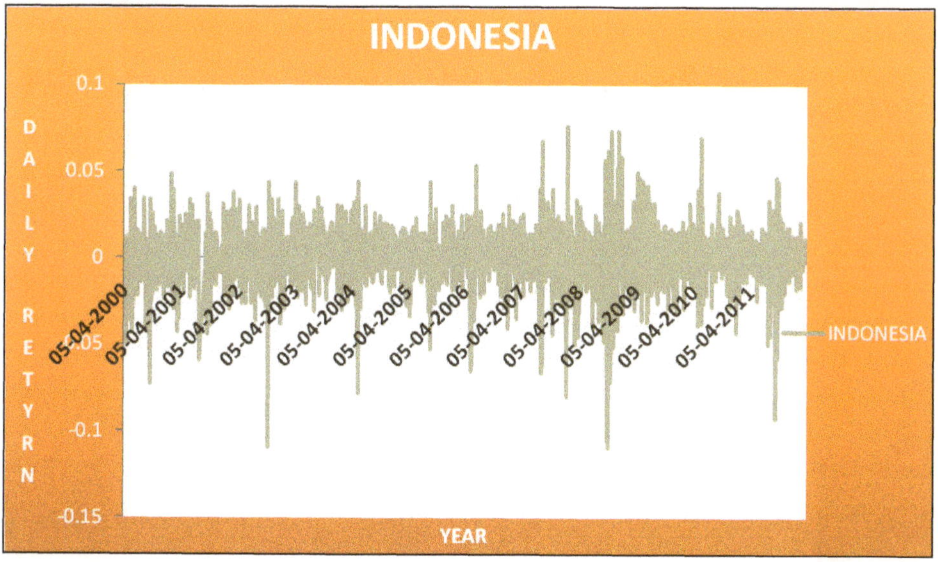

Figure 5.2: Stock Index Daily Average Return Indonesia (2000 – 2012).

disturbances in major financial markets, in particular in U.S, Europe and Asia where stock exchanges indices fell dramatically at historical levels. From that period on, governments had taken measures to ensure the stability of the financial system until the end of 2009. But at that time, the overall global economy does not recover since financial crisis impacts on real economic variables such us GDP growth, inflation and unemployment (among others) were higher. In the year 2010-2011 all the countries return was positive except Japan and China, but in the year 2011-2012 all the countries return was negative except Japan, Indonesia, Kola Lumpur and US. In India Exports have grown by 29.4 per cent, while imports have recorded a

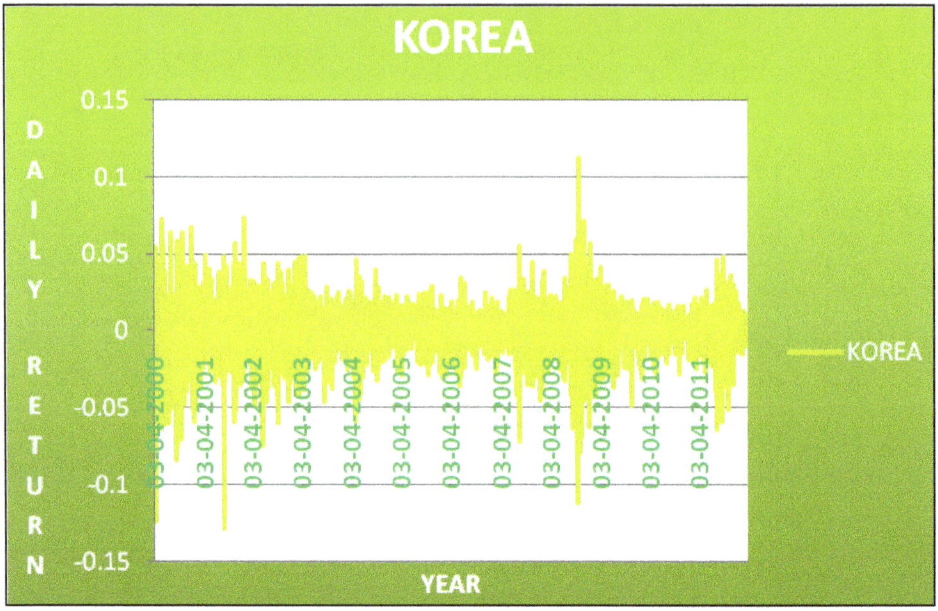

Figure 5.3: Stock Index Daily Average Return Korea (2000 – 2012).

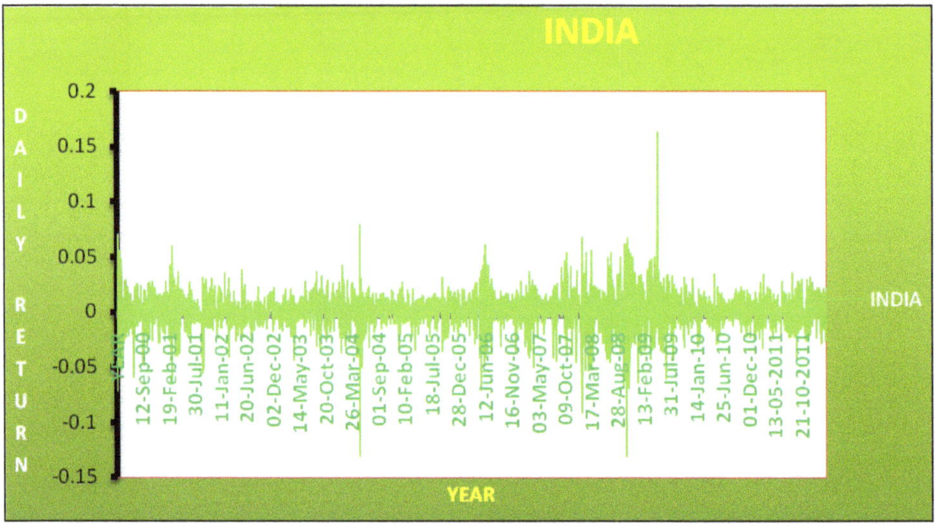

Figure 5.4: Stock Index Daily Average Return India (2000 – 2012).

growth of 17.6 per cent during April to January 2010-11 over the corresponding period last year.

In the year 2003-2004, 2005-2006 and 2006-2007 all the countries enjoyed positive return. Among all the countries, China's return was high (0.3753) in the year 2006 – 2007, compared to other markets. In India and Indonesia the return was very high in the year 2003-2004 and in the year 2009-2010. In the year 2002-2003 France experienced severe loss (–0.2254). In 2007 – 2008 the return was high

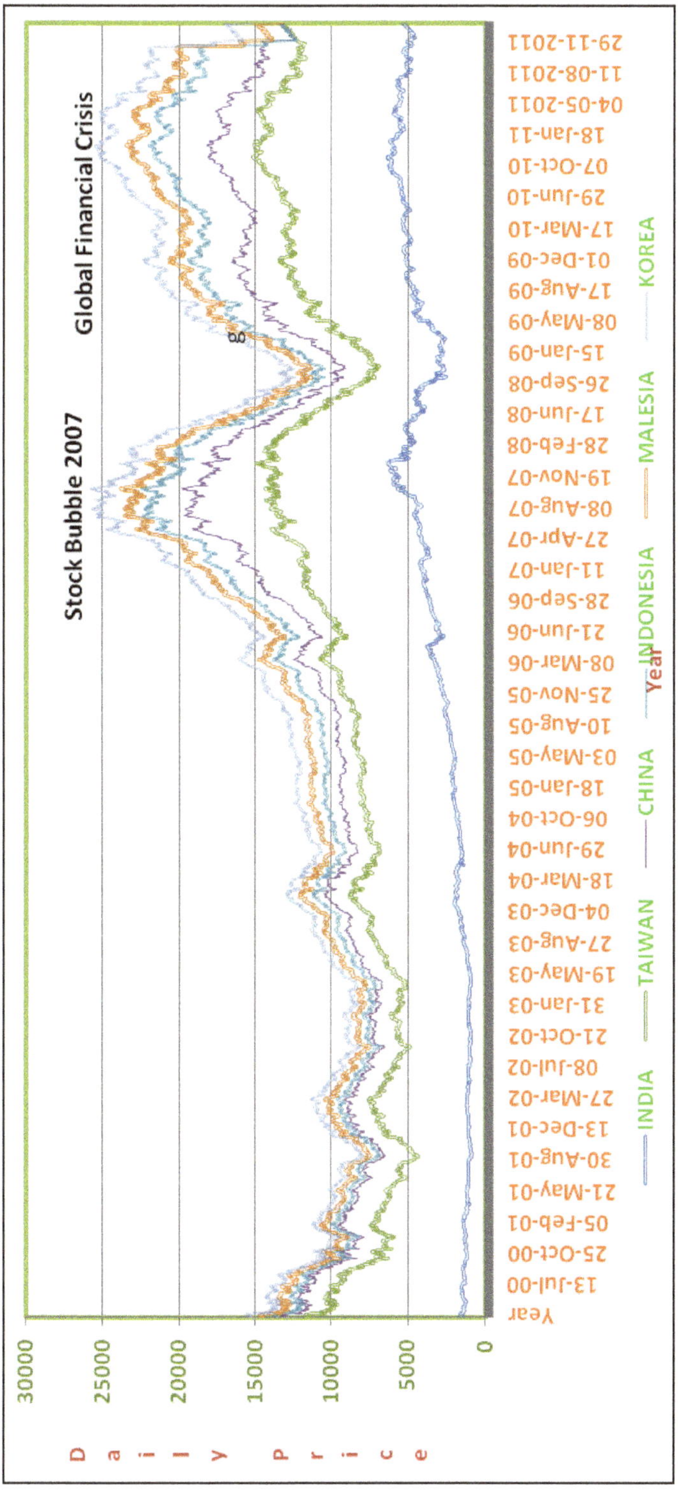

Figure 5.5: Daily Stock Price Movement in Developing Countries (2000 – 2012).

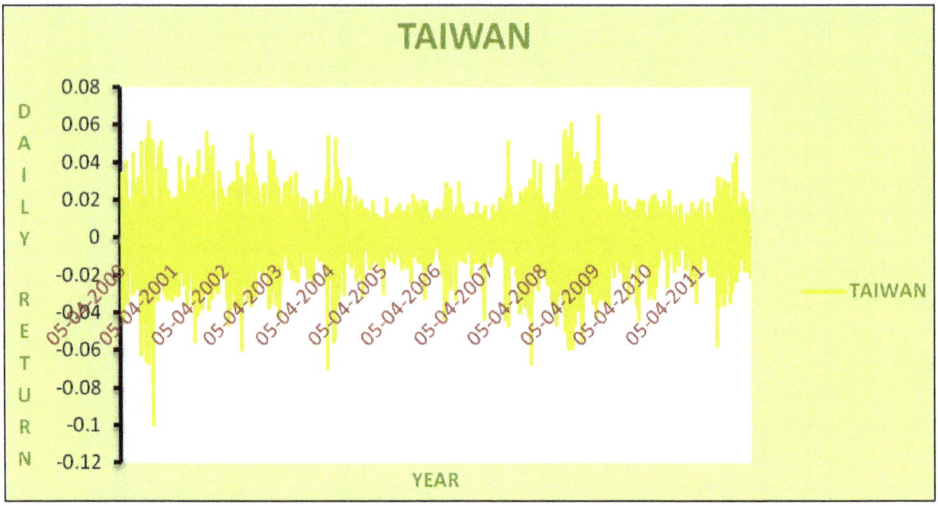

Figure 5.6: Stock Index Daily Average Return Taiwan (2000 – 2012).

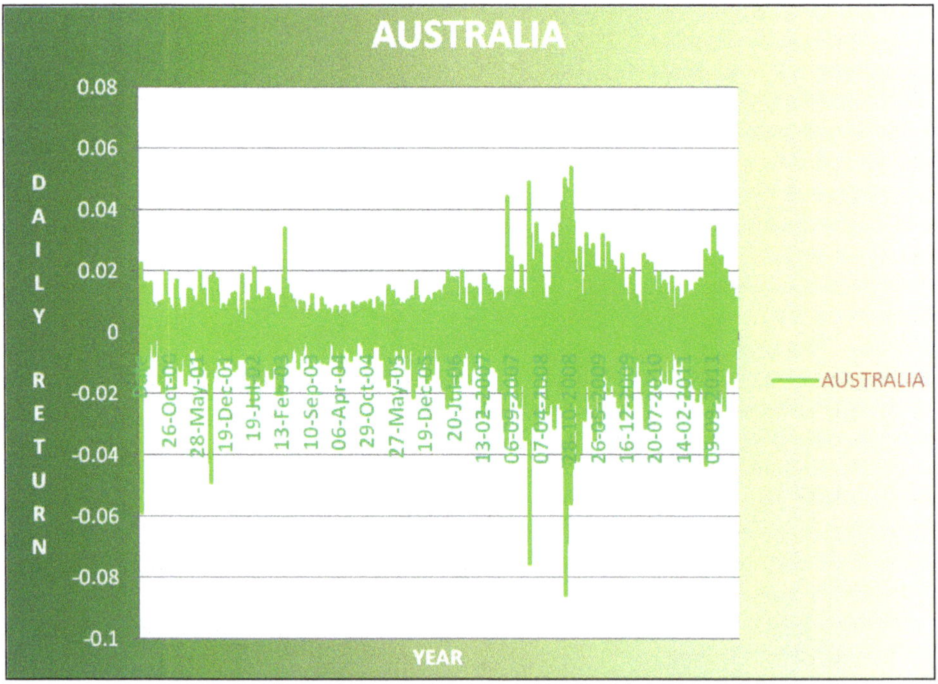

Figure 5.7: Stock Index Daily Average Return Australia (2000 – 2012).

in Indonesia and India. In January 8, 2008, the Nifty reached the peak of 6287.25 points the market was favoured by domestic Institutional Investors and FIIs. The market valuation, the Reliance Communication, Reliance Energy, Sterlite and Unitech commanded rich P/E multiplies. But the market could not keep the gains

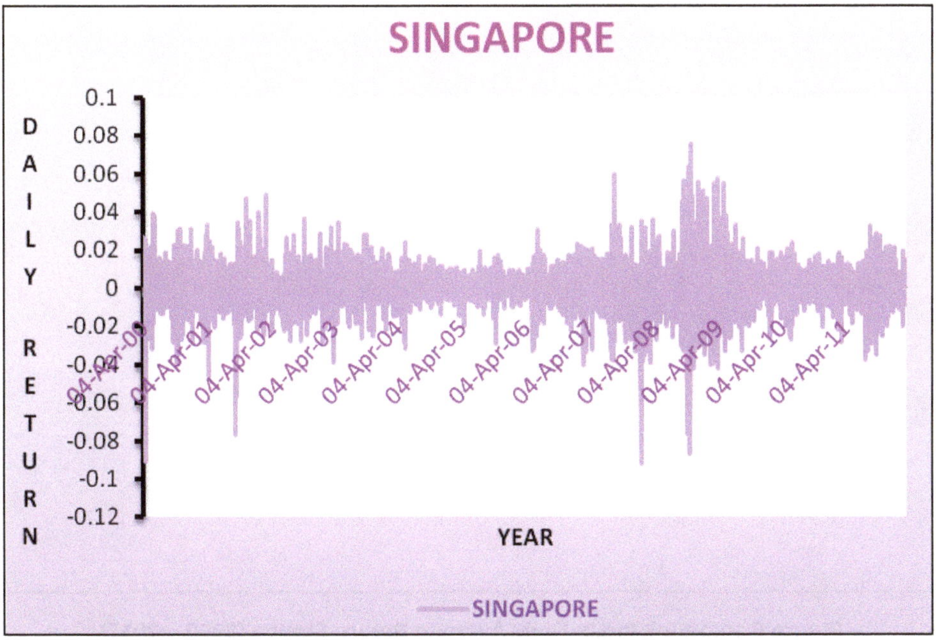

Figure 5.8: Stock Index Daily Average Return Singapore (2000 – 2012).

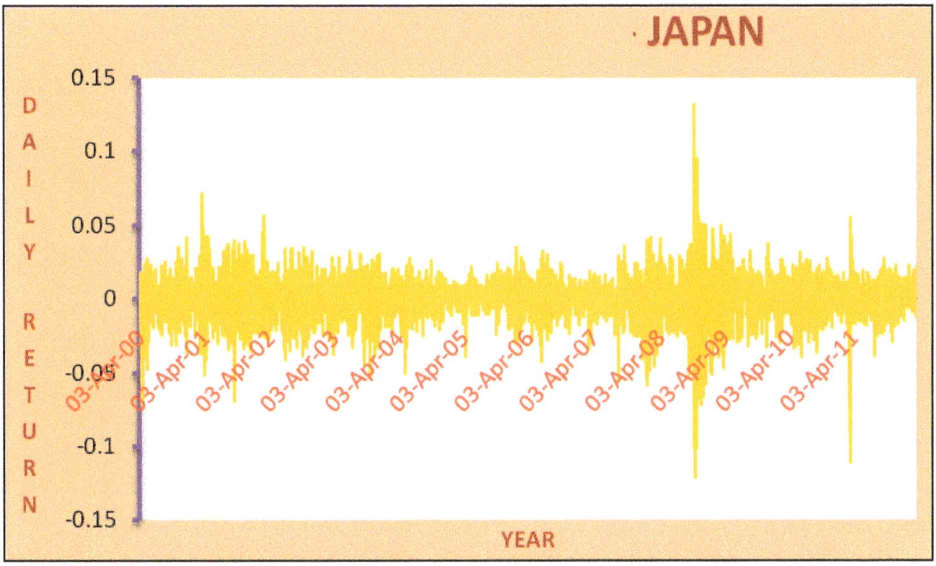

Figure 5.9: Stock Index Daily Average Return Japan (2000 – 2012).

for a long time. The reason for this was global outlook, and liquidity sucked out by the two IPOs namely Reliance Power and Future Capital. However, unprecedented events of an unimaginable scale in the Wall Street in mid-September 2008, abruptly and completely changed the course of economic policy debate as well as immediate

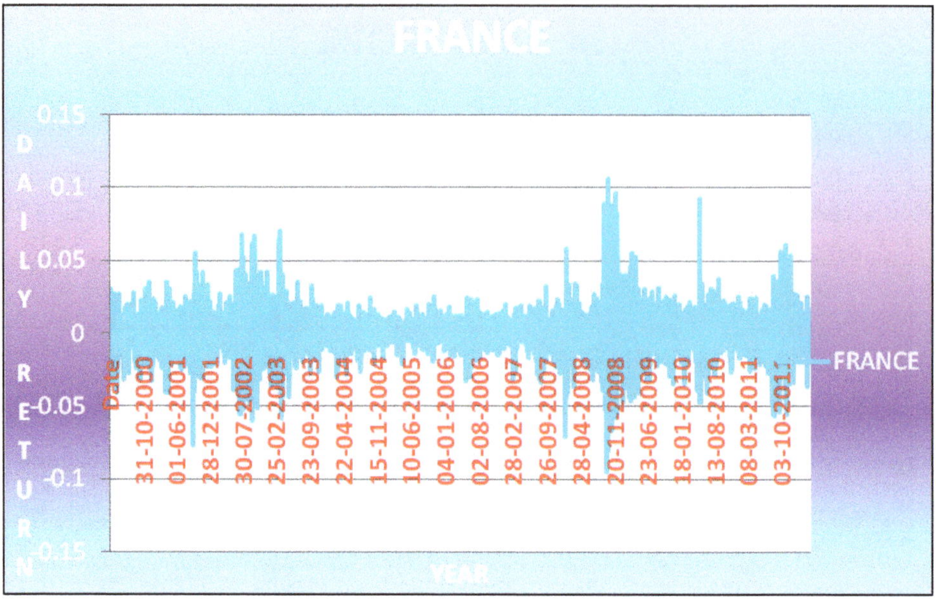

Figure 5.10: Stock Index Daily Average Return France (2000 – 2012).

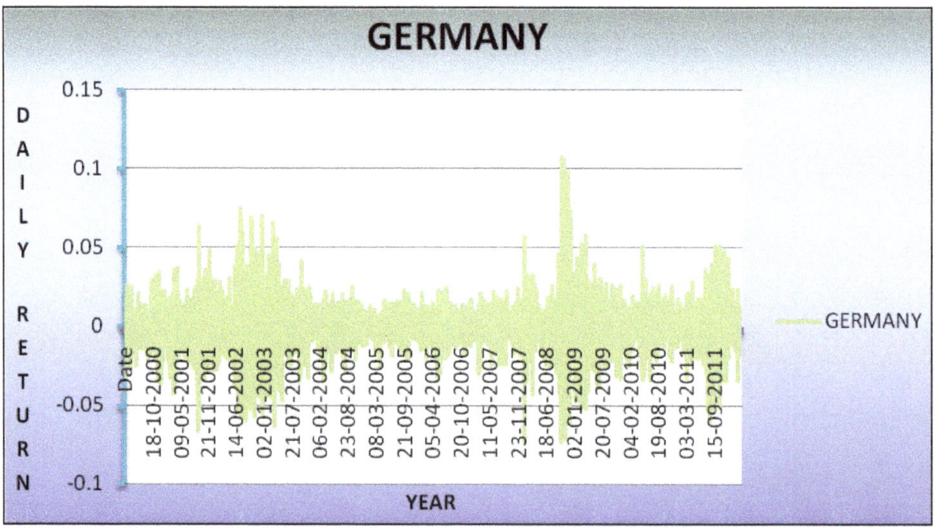

Figure 5.11: Stock Index Daily Average Return Germany (2000 – 2012).

prospects for the world economy. The early bankruptcy of Bears Steams and its takeover by JP Morgan-Chase in March 2008 and the collapse of other banks and financial institutions in the United States and Europe indicated the depth of the crisis and credit freeze impeding the normal operation of financial markets in these economies. In early September, the government of the United States sponsored mortgage buyout of Freddie Mac and Fannie Mae, which together accounted for

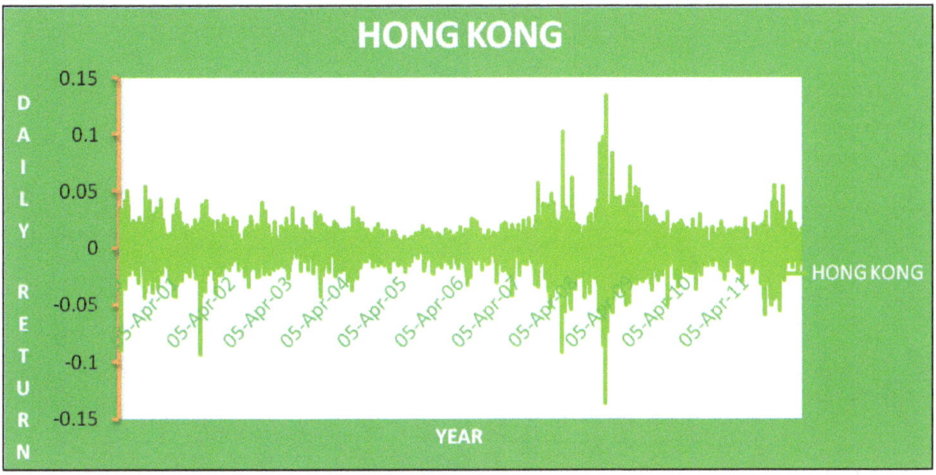

Figure 5.12: Stock Index Daily Average Return Hong Kong (2000 – 2012).

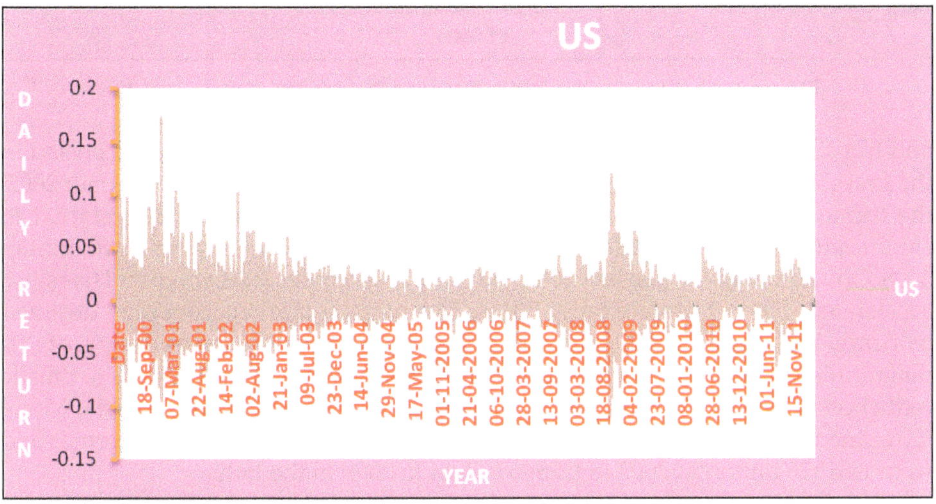

Figure 5.13: Stock Index Daily Average Return US (2000 – 2012).

some half of United States mortgage loans, amounting to $5 trillion. The two were practically nationalized after the early rescue package failed to shore them up. After that, the bankruptcy of Lehman Brothers - one of the four big Wall Street investment banks – immediately followed by the take-over of Merrill Lynch by Bank of America and a $85 billion rescue package hastily arranged for American Insurance Group (AIG) which made everyone wake up to the scale of the problems on the Wall Street.

Emerging stock market, measured by the Morgan Stanley Composite Index (MSCI), fell by more than 60 per cent between mid-September and mid-November 2008 shows that MSCI fell sharply in emerging market economies in all regions. Equity markets in emerging markets have not experienced a recovery as much as those in developed economies in the first quarter of 2009. Equity prices in China

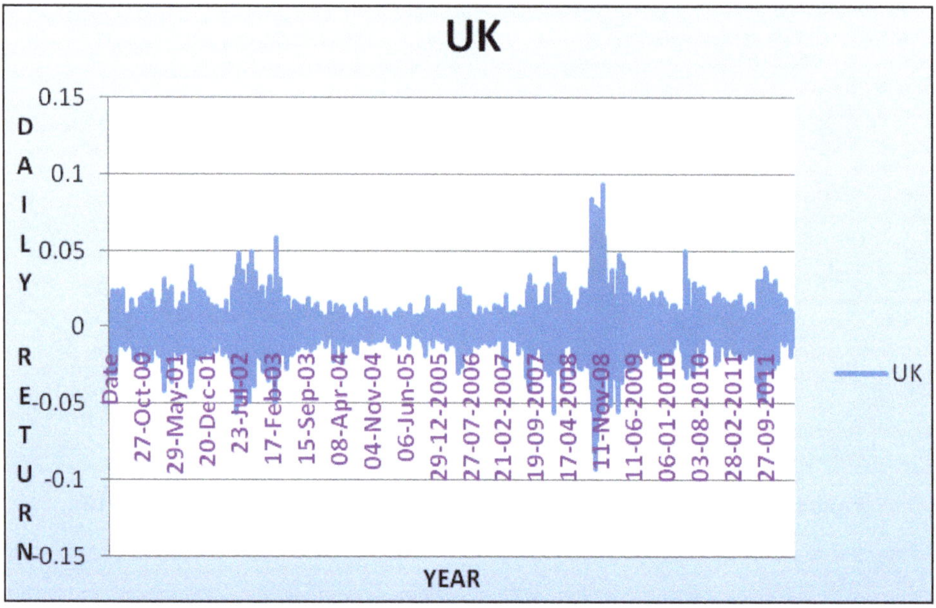

Figure 5.14: Stock Index Daily Average Return UK (2000 – 2012).

and India all posted a drop by over 60 per cent. Despite some resilience posted in the first six months after the initial outbreak of the financial crisis, in summer 2007, the turmoil continued and intensified in major financial centres. This started to significantly affect private debt and equity capital flows to emerging economies in 2008. On account of the marked deterioration in September 2008, this trend has since accelerated. The net private capital flows to emerging market economies declined by nearly half, from US$929 billion in 2007 to $466 billion in 2008. A decline of this magnitude was observed across all categories of private capital flows. The drastic reduction appears to have occurred in emerging market economies in Asia, where it declined from US$184 billion in 2007 to US$89 billion in 2008 in the former and from US$315 billion in 2007 to US$96 billion in 2008 in the latter.

In Hong-Kong the return was very high in the year 2009-2010 followed by the global financial crisis. Before the global financial crisis all the all the countries had positive return except Japan. According to the World Bank (2009), since mid-September, currencies of developing countries had declined by more than 20 per cent by November. Some currencies that had appreciated strongly for two years before summer 2008 experienced a larger depreciation in the immediate aftermath.

Only India, Korea, Indonesia and Kola Lumpur earned positive return before crisis after the crisis and the whole study period. According to the estimates of the Institute of International Finance, released at the end of January 2009, net private capital flows to emerging market economies was sustained for several years and accelerated from $565 billion in 2006 to a high level of nearly $929 billion in 2007 of which $518 billion is known to have flowed to BRICs. Thus, initially, emerging market economies as a group appeared to have weathered the storm of the financial

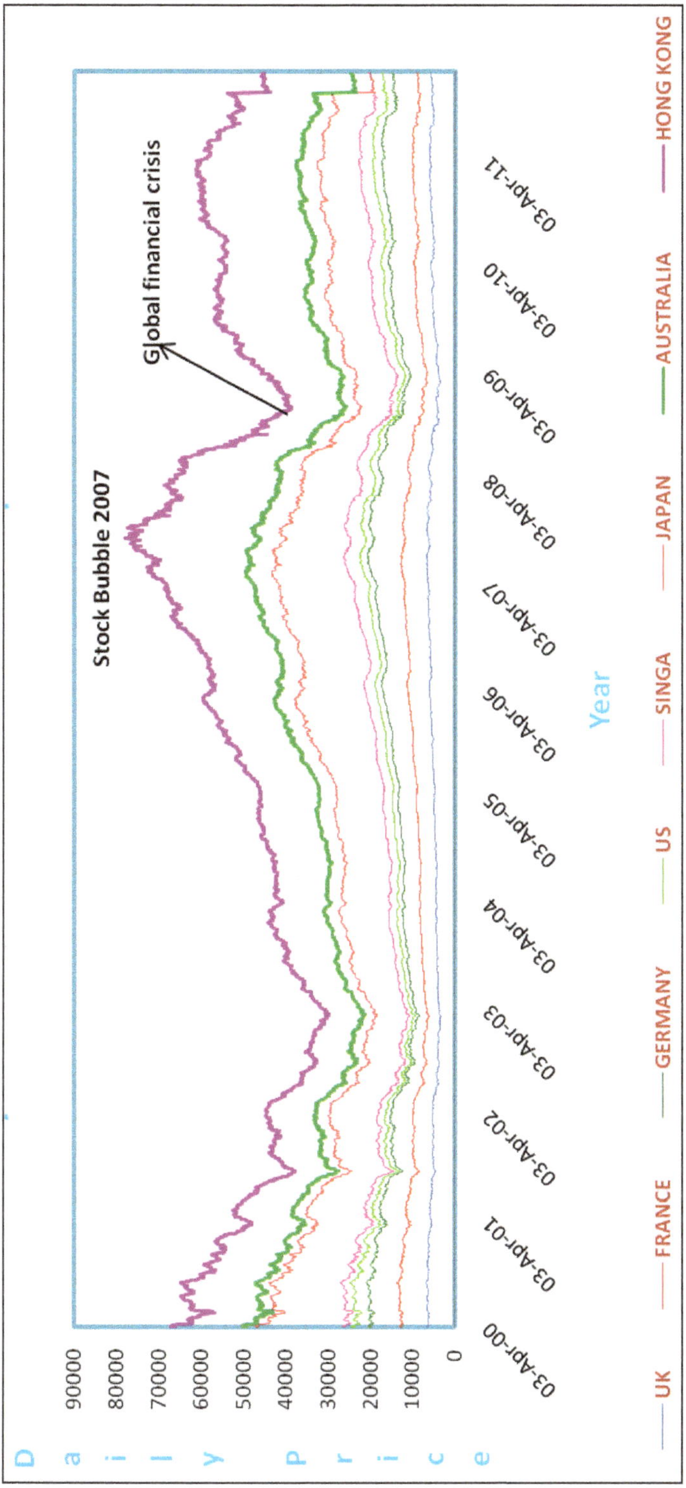

Figure 5.15: Daily Stock Price Movement in Developed Countries (2000 – 2012).

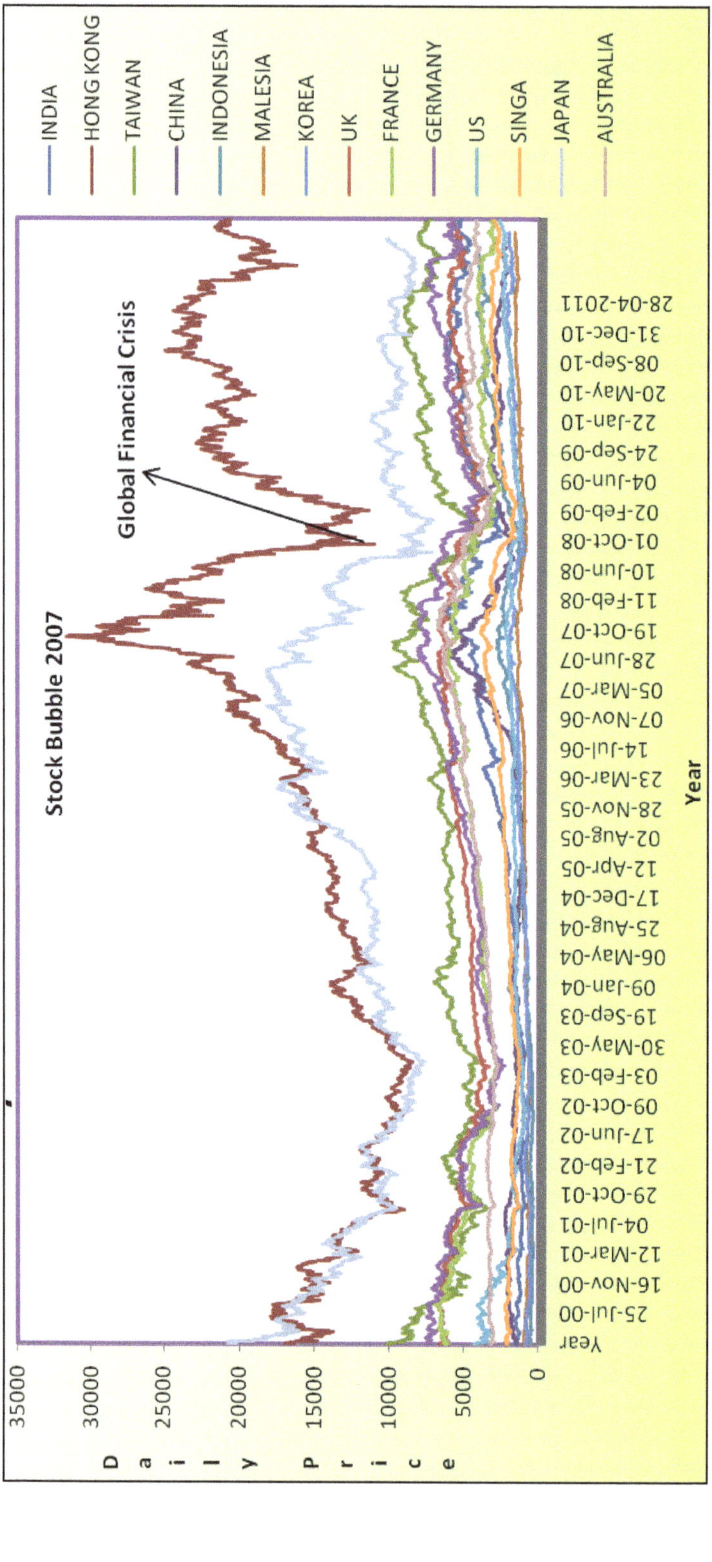

Figure 5.16: Daily Stock Price Movement for all the Countries (2000 – 2012).

markets of the United States and Western Europe throughout 2007. Japan return was negative in all the three phases. Scarce in many natural resources, Japan has long been dependent on imported raw materials. Since the complete shutdown of Japan's nuclear reactors after the earthquake and tsunami disaster in 2011, Japan's industrial sector has become even more dependent than it was previously on imported fossil fuels. Modest economic growth continued after 2000, but the economy has fallen into recession four times since 2008. Government stimulus spending helped the economy recover in late 2009 and 2010, but the economy contracted again in 2011 as the massive 9.0 magnitude earthquake and the ensuing tsunami in March of that year disrupted manufacturing.

Compared to emerging markets, developed markets suffered loss for several years. Japan suffered loss for seven years. An analysis of the average returns shows that all the developed countries except Hong Kong and US registered negative average returns in the year 2007-08. All the macro economic factors had a negative impact on the return of selected countries stocks. Bond issuance by emerging market economies decreased to US$72 billion in October 2008, from US$170 billion in June 2007. Corporate bond issuance fell by US$15.6 billion in South Africa, US$12.8 billion in India and US$9.4 billion in Russia, whereas equity issuance posted a similar fall. Most currencies of emerging and developing countries have experienced a sharp depreciation.

In particular, Asian economies have turned out to be most vulnerable to the recessionary impact of the financial crisis, as global trade collapsed in the final quarter of 2008 due to their heavy reliance on export demand, in particular for manufactured goods. These Asian economies have been hit particularly hard because of the sharp drop in global demand for consumer durables, such as automobiles, electronics and capital goods, where their specialization of manufacturing exports lies. Many companies in India began to use measures such as sabbaticals and shorter working weeks to cut production and postpone lay-offs of workers. Industries such as automobiles were also hit hard. While the sharpest decline was reported in construction and textiles, in October, car sales dropped by nearly 20 per cent in November - the worst fall for India in eight years. In December, the industrial grouping of jute and other vegetable fibre textiles except cotton, recorded a negative growth of 66.4 per cent, followed by the negative growth rates of 20 per cent in wood and wood products; furniture and fixtures and 17.9 per cent in transport equipment and parts.

Among all the countries Korea had high volatility for six years. Global financial crisis has negatively affected volatility of Australia, Germany, UK, Singapore, Japan and Hong Kong stock market adversely, the volatility of these markets were at its peak in 2008-09. One interesting fact is that emerging markets were not immediately affected by the global financial crisis. All the emerging markets earned positive return in the year 2007-2008, whereas in the developed countries except Hong Kong and US, other markets suffered loss in the year 2007-2008. In the year 2000-2001, 2002-2003 and 2008-2009 all the countries both emerging markets and developed markets threw up negative returns and in these years by and large the volatilities have been bigger than immediate preceding years. In the year 2000-2001 the loss was very high in USA (–0.393), in 2002-2003 the loss was very high in France (–0.3151), in the year 2008-09 the loss was very high in Singapore (–0.2254). In the year 2000-2001, except Australia and Singapore all the developed markets experienced loss, in emerging markets only China and India experienced loss in 2001-2002. In 2003 the volatility slowed down in almost all the countries which is analysed in this sample. Australia provided low return with low volatility. Tables 5.5–5.8 provide statistics pertaining to asymmetrics such as skewness and kurtosis (higher order moments).

Table 5.5: Higher Order Moments of Stock Index Daily Returns (Emerging Countries China, Indonesia and Kola Lumpur)

Year	*China*		*Indonesia*		*Kola Lumpur*	
	Skew	*kurt*	*Skew*	*kurt*	*Skew*	*kurt*
2000-2001	–1.169	2.946	–0.501	2.451	–0.481	2.842
2001-2002	0.588	6.369	–0.499	2.386	–1.123	5.626
2002-2003	1.891	10.845	–1.292	10.087	0.239	1.635
2003-2004	0.425	0.529	0.204	0.396	0.323	0.977
2004-2005	0.727	1.424	–1.050	6.575	–0.107	1.503
2005-2006	1.936	12.897	–0.321	2.358	0.357	1.716
2006-2007	–1.102	4.519	–0.294	1.367	0.126	7.666
2007-2008	–0.886	2.410	–0.632	4.423	–2.274	16.591
2008-2009	0.212	0.767	–0.484	4.405	0.111	1.504
2009-2010	–0.768	4.718	0.1689	3.719	0.0454	40.383
2010-2011	–0.671	4.735	0.1325	6.655	–0.5295	4.3791
2011-2012	0.046	3.813	–1.610	12.626	–0.3186	4.379
2000–2012	–0.092	7.6117	–0.7136	9.1280.	–0.2697	9.169

The kurtosis of the normal distribution is 3. If the kurtosis exceeds 3 the distribution is peaked (leptokurtic) relative to the normal, if the kurtosis is less than 3 the distribution is flat (playtykurtic) relative to the normal. The skewness of a symmetric distribution is zero. Positive skewness means that the distribution has a long right tail, while negative skewness means that the distributions have a long left tail.

Table 5.6: Higher Order Moments of Stock Index Daily Returns (Emerging Countries Korea, India and Taiwan)

Year	*Korea*		*India*		*Taiwan*	
	Skew	*kurt*	*Skew*	*kurt*	*Skew*	*kurt*
2000-2001	–0.247	1.277	–0.282	1.577	–0.108	0.996
2001-2002	–0.815	6.627	–0.571	2.409	0.229	0.056
2002-2003	–0.146	0.175	0.091	0.725	0.189	0.530
2003-2004	–0.194	1.025	–0.349	0.122	–0.436	4.188
2004-2005	–0.496	1.575	–2.263	19.739	–0.430	3.092

Contd...

Table 5.6–*Contd...*

Year	Korea		India		Taiwan	
	Skew	*kurt*	*Skew*	*kurt*	*Skew*	*kurt*
2005-2006	−0.517	0.529	−0.634	0.842	−0.273	1.054
2006-2007	−0.348	0.995	−0.474	1.662	−0.957	3.078
2007-2008	−0.626	1.968	−0.497	2.847	−0.656	1.911
2008-2009	−0.320	3.804	−0.357	1.815	−0.038	0.510
2009-2010	−0.533	7.935	2.459	21.670	0.0375	5.743
2010-2011	−0.428	3.268	−0.0882	0.326	−0.715	4.298
2011-2012	−0.392	4.732	0.1783	−0.044	−.0.253	4.588
2000–2012	−0.537	7.935	−0.2802	7.504	−0.233	5.392

The kurtosis of the normal distribution is 3. If the kurtosis exceeds 3 the distribution is peaked (leptokurtic) relative to the normal, if the kurtosis is less than 3 the distribution is flat (playtykurtic) relative to the normal. The skewness of a symmetric distribution is zero. Positive skewness means that the distribution has a long right tail, while negative skewness means that the distributions have a long left tail.

Table 5.7: Higher Order Moments of Stock Index Daily Returns (Developed Countries Australia, Singapore and Japan)

Year	Australia		Singapore		Japan	
	Skew	*kurt*	*Skew*	*kurt*	*Skew*	*kurt*
2000-2001	−1.465	10.334	−0.812	4.948	0.078	3.050
2001-2002	−1.445	8.715	−0.554	4.872	0.163	0.695
2002-2003	0.294	1.352	0.123	0.737	−0.002	−0.310
2003-2004	−0.044	0.086	0.035	0.278	−0.578	0.964
2004-2005	−0.382	0.625	−0.531	2.179	−0.464	1.821
2005-2006	−0.624	0.902	−0.619	2.821	−0.258	0.977
2006-2007	−0.462	0.566	−0.783	1.791	−0.390	1.006
2007-2008	−0.442	3.842	−0.814	4.945	−0.521	1.430
2008-2009	−0.329	1.851	0.037	2.048	−0.217	3.779
2009-2010	−0.161	3.367	0.5716	5.238	0.0961	0.372
2010 -2011	−0.186	3.538	−0.297	3.929	−1.4670	10.099
2011- 2012	−0.158	3.665	−0.350	3.965	−0.1454	−0.222
2000–2012	−0.611	9.389	−.0406	8.728	−0.3924	6.599

The kurtosis of the normal distribution is 3. If the kurtosis exceeds 3 the distribution is peaked (leptokurtic) relative to the normal, if the kurtosis is less than 3 the distribution is flat (playtykurtic) relative to the normal. The skewness of a symmetric distribution is zero. Positive skewness means that the distribution

Table 5.8: Higher Order Moments of Stock Index Daily Returns (Developed Countries France, Germany, Hong-Kong US and UK)

Year	France		Germany		Hong-Kong		US		UK	
	Mean	Std	Mean	Std	Mean	Std	Mean	Std	Mean	Std
2000-2001	0.017	–0.166	–0.119	–0.214	–0.234	2.061	0.506	1.397	–0.239	0.074
2001-2002	–0.190	1.602	–0.287	2.364	–0.460	3.135	0.347	0.661	–0.067	2.889
2002-2003	0.308	–0.056	0.320	0.262	0.368	0.502	0.443	0.136	–0.102	63.180
2003-2004	0.135	1.229	–0.138	4.299	–0.037	1.221	0.053	0.028	0.009	2.454
2004-2005	–0.282	0.658	–0.265	0.749	–0.091	1.605	–0.108	–0.264	–0.322	0.203
2005-2006	–0.302	0.654	–0.077	0.601	–0.468	0.885	–0.135	1.361	0.188	–0.013
2006-2007	–0.493	0.924	–0.449	0.931	–0.603	1.183	–0.094	1.205	–0.435	0.022
2007-2008	–0.631	5.585	–0.354	3.532	–0.034	2.938	–0.142	0.488	–0.131	1.557
2008-2009	0.516	4.190	0.376	3.378	0.271	3.846	0.140	2.590	0.101	53.472
2009-2010	–0.133	3.585	0.0036	3.934	0.337	3.926	–0.3637	1.141	–0.1281	3.595
2010 -2011	0.5800	9.116	0.0376	4.885	–0.263	3.056	–0.2372	2.241	0.1316	4.806
2011- 2012	–0.150	4.452	–0.124	4.122	–0.206	4.937	–04540	5.564	–0.2496	4.334
2000–2012	0.426	7.745	0.0426	7.025	–0.029	10.685	0.2365	5.434	–0.1194	8.808

The kurtosis of the normal distribution is 3. if the kurtosis exceeds 3 the distribution is peaked (leptokurtic) relative to the normal, if the kurtosis is less than 3 the distribution is flat (playtykurtic) relative to the normal. The skewness of a symmetric distribution is zero.

has a long right tail, while negative skewness means that the distributions have a long left tail.

Positive skewness means that the distribution has a long right tail, while negative skewness means that the distributions have a long left tail

For any data to be random, the first assumption is that it should possess the characteristics of a normal distribution. An important property of a normal distribution is that the skewness and kurtosis must be equal to 0 and 3 respectively. A look at Tables 5.5–5.8 reveal that both the distributions are not normal. Therefore as per this technique, none of the stock markets follow the theory of random walk as the distributions are not normal. The value of Kurtosis is greater than the standard 3 in the series, and then they have a heavier tail than the standard normal distribution. The daily stock returns are, thus, not normally distributed. There is a clear pattern available between developed capital markets and emerging capital markets overtime. Among developed markets UK has had very high kurtosis, in that order, apart from negative skewness.

India experienced very high kurtosis in the year 2004 – 2005 due to national factors and in the year 2009-10 due to global financial crisis. Majority of the developed countries experienced high kurtosis in the year 2007- 2008 to 2011-2012. Emerging markets had highest Kurtosis in the year 2009 – 2010 among them Kola Lumpur had highest Kurtosis (40.383) and among the developed markets it was very high in UK in the year 2008- 2009.

Table 5.9: Stock Index Daily Close to Close and Open to Open Volatility (percentage (Emerging Countries China, Indonesia and Kola Lumpur)

Year	*China*		*Indonesia*		*Kola Lumpur*	
	Close-close	*Open-open*	*Close-close*	*Open-open*	*Close-close*	*Open-open*
2000-2001	0.996	1.077	1.530	1.550	1.244	1.209
2001-2002	1.672	1.916	1.349	1.254	1.269	1.272
2002-2003	1.274	1.434	1.508	1.445	0.808	0.780
2003-2004	1.129	1.205	1.238	1.273	0.734	0.748
2004-2005	1.310	1.400	1.288	1.243	0.644	0.651
2005-2006	1.475	1.469	1.166	1.211	0.465	0.463
2006-2007	1.738	2.030	1.344	1.418	0.800	0.829
2007-2008	2.395	2.526	1.805	1.942	1.251	1.145
2008-2009	2.752	3.092	2.304	2.711	1.135	1.216
2009-2010	1.72	1.847	1.440	1.433	2.6153	2.663
2010 -2011	1.416	1.537	1.319	1.313	0.563	0.599
2011- 2012	1.193	1.244	1.401	1.397	0.693	0.657
2000–2012	1.686	1.837	1.510	1.576	1.164	1.170

Table 5.10: Stock Index Daily Close to Close and Open to Open Volatility (percentage) (Emerging Countries Korea, India and Taiwan)

Year	*Korea*		*India*		*Taiwan*	
	Close-close	*Open-open*	*Close-close*	*Open-open*	*Close-close*	*Open-open*
2000-2001	2.866	3.021	1.984	1.979	2.374	2.611
2001-2002	2.052	2.180	1.404	1.445	1.917	2.315
2002-2003	2.060	2.058	0.992	0.998	1.773	1.940
2003-2004	1.376	1.509	1.433	1.454	1.307	1.476
2004-2005	1.488	1.467	1.641	1.648	1.325	1.301
2005-2006	1.106	1.220	1.036	1.042	0.859	0.937
2006-2007	1.086	1.141	1.776	1.798	1.055	1.021
2007-2008	1.629	1.712	2.025	1.998	1.585	1.689
2008-2009	2.554	2.758	2.664	2.656	2.095	2.570
2009-2010	1.763	1.263	1.882	1.879	1.404	1.515
2010 -2011	0.944	1.030	1.118	1.087	0.989	1.073
2011- 2012	1.642	1.643	1.301	1.431	1.352	1.382
2000–2012	1.763	1.849	1.670	1.680	1.567	1.742

Table 5.11: Stock Index Daily Close to Close and Open to Open Volatility (percentage) (Developed Countries Australia, Singapore and Japan)

Year	*Australia*		*Singapore*		*Japan*	
	Close-close	*Open-open*	*Close-close*	*Open-open*	*Close-close*	*Open-open*
2000-2001	0.808	0.816	1.481	1.414	1.616	1.491
2001-2002	0.783	0.787	1.443	1.588	1.826	1.563
2002-2003	0.770	0.771	1.120	1.204	1.531	1.386
2003-2004	0.468	0.453	1.028	1.144	1.368	1.306
2004-2005	0.425	0.402	0.718	0.680	1.057	1.013
2005-2006	0.629	0.582	0.598	0.597	1.081	1.071
2006-2007	0.848	0.762	1.042	1.069	1.147	1.088
2007-2008	1.402	1.220	1.587	1.714	1.565	1.313
2008-2009	1.942	1.713	2.204	2.180	2.936	2.494
2009-2010	1.121	0.969	1.325	1.322	1.421	1.160
2010 -2011	0.929	0.822	0.841	0.839	1.594	1.439
2011- 2012	1.121	1.057	1.133	1.137	1.141	1.079
2000–2012	1.030	0.929	1.280	1.312	1.600	1.421

India and Taiwan experienced experienced negative skewness in the year 2003 – 2004 to 2008- 2009 and Indonesia experienced had negative skewness from 2004 to 2008 – 2009. Both developed and emerging markets had negative skewness in the year 2007 – 2008. Reasons for this behavior include global financial crisis in the US

Table 5.12: Stock Index Daily Close to Close and Open to Open Volatility (percentage) (Developed Countries France, Germany, Hong-Kong US and UK)

Year	*France*		*Germany*		*Hong-Kong*		*US*		*UK*	
	Close-close	*Open-open*	*Close-close*	*Open-open*	*Close-close*	*Open-open*	*Close-close*	*Open-open*	*Close-close*	*Open-open*
2000-2001	1.442	1.422	1.424	1.615	1.801	1.737	3.878	4.015	1.164	1.165
2001-2002	1.754	1.811	1.576	1.646	1.704	1.498	2.917	3.034	1.225	1.291
2002-2003	2.783	2.715	2.450	2.451	1.167	1.224	2.683	2.794	1.921	1.916
2003-2004	1.494	1.473	1.165	1.248	1.063	1.178	1.387	1.401	0.860	0.876
2004-2005	0.886	0.860	0.789	0.741	0.962	0.933	1.111	1.058	0.598	0.597
2005-2006	0.811	0.757	0.724	0.723	0.721	0.755	0.864	0.815	0.584	0.581
2006-2007	0.996	0.907	0.968	0.982	1.043	1.077	1.007	0.997	0.843	0.844
2007-2008	1.316	1.335	1.390	1.656	2.192	2.047	1.410	1.459	1.375	1.360
2008-2009	2.454	2.328	2.587	2.599	3.056	3.369	2.806	2.605	2.399	2.383
2009-2010	1.421	1.394	1.422	0.0133	1.714	1.632	1.182	1.133	1.130	1.159
2010 -2011	1.594	1.446	1.142	0.968	1.080	1.083	1.186	1.202	1.107	1.106
2011- 2012	1.141	1.947	1.851	2.011	1.613	1.590	1.448	1.321	1.329	1.329
2000–2012	1.600	1.639	1.639	0.6481	1.634	1.652	2.051	2.066	1.312	1.316

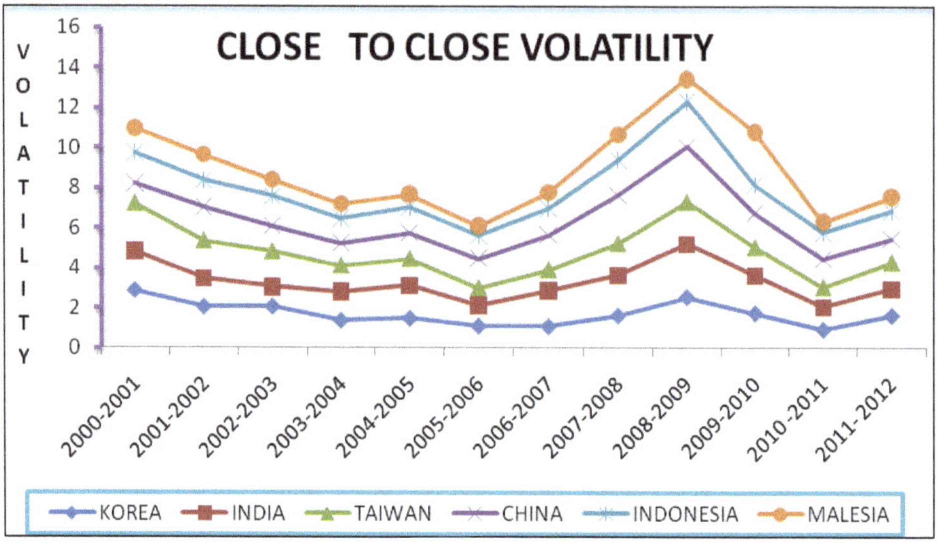

Figure 5.17: Close to Close Volatility for Developing Countries (2000 – 2012).

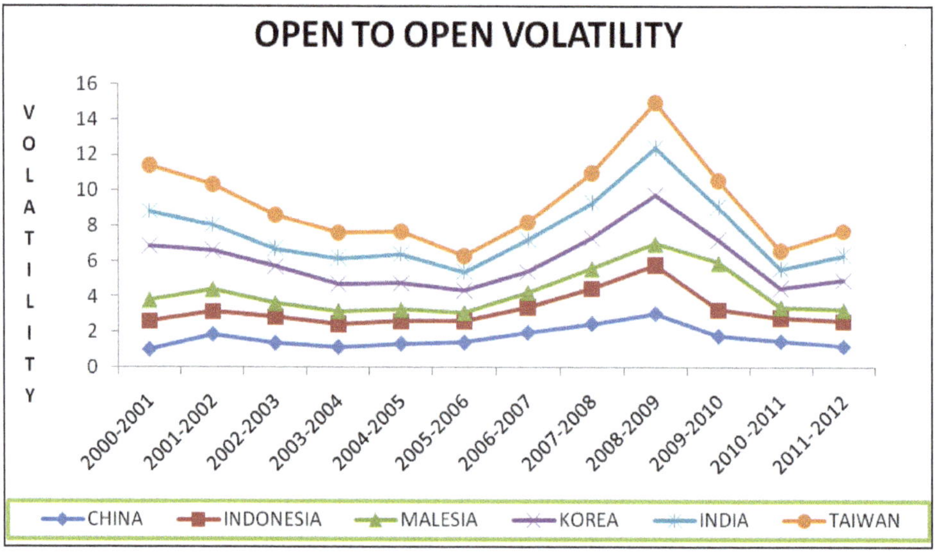

Figure 5.18: Open to Open Volatility for Developing Countries (2000 – 2012).

stock markets and its contagion effect on some of the markets. Except 2002 – 2003 Australian market followed negative skewness. France, Germany, Hong –Kong, US and UK had negative skewness from 2004- 2005 to 2007 – 2008. This indicated that the stock Index returns were getting increasingly concentrated at higher ranges, which is a very good sign. A positive skewness means that returns were falling and were concentrated in low range. During the study period 2000-12 all the countries had negative skewness except France, Germany and US returns.

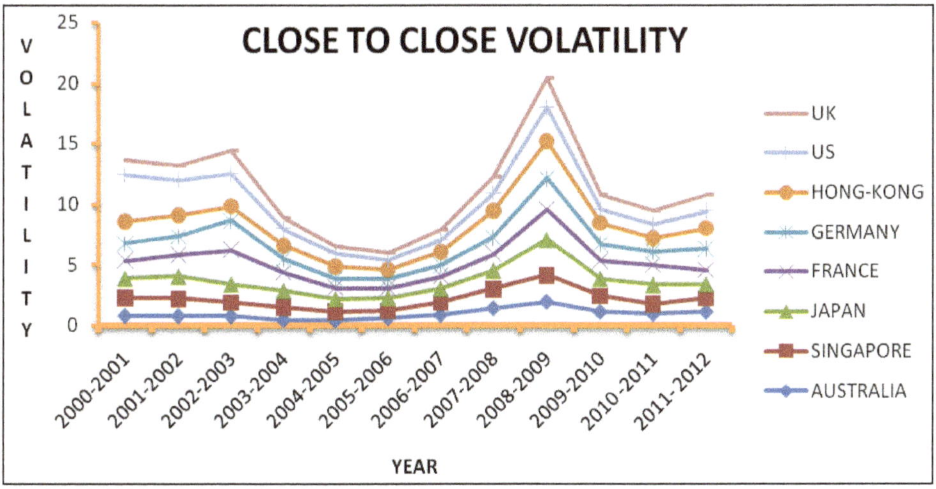

Figure 5.19: Close to Close Volatility for Developed Countries (2000 – 2012).

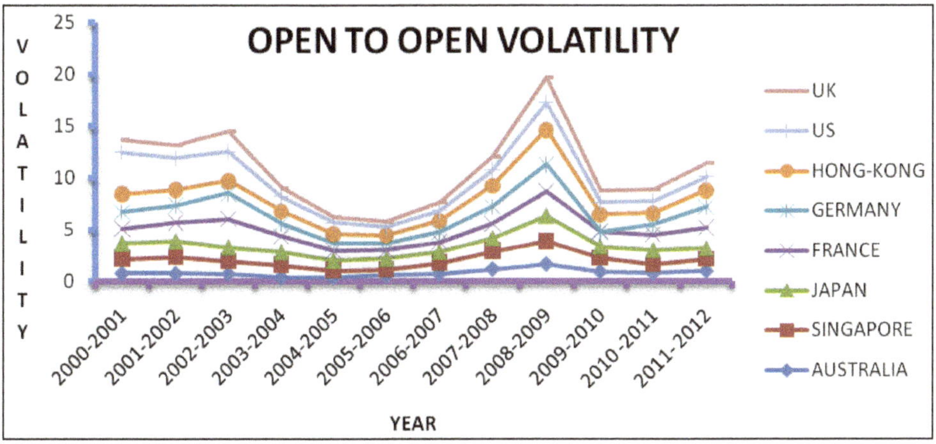

Figure 5.20: Open to Open Volatility for Developed Countries (2000 – 2012).

In India, open to open and close to close volatility appears to be neck to neck. This indicates smooth flow of information during the day as well as over -night. In China, Indonesia, and India the interday volatility was very high in the year 2007 -2008 and 2008 – 2009. It touched its 3 per centage points in China and in Hong-Kong in 2008 – 2009. In the developed countries except Australia interday volatility was very high in the year 20008 - 2009. It clearly exhibits that developed countries moved in tandem with each other. Intraday and inter day movements in stock prices appears to have considerably stable in Australia. Interday volatility has been consistently lower than 1 per cent and it is less than half per cent in 2003 – 2004 and 2004 – 2005. Among emerging markets volatility was very low in Indonesia, Kola Lumpur and Taiwan in the year 2005 -2006. In India the interday volatility was very low in the year 2002 – 2003. In Japan and Australia the interday volatility was very low in the year 2004 – 2005. From the year 2003 -2004 to 2008 – 2009 developed markets exhibit the same pattern in the open to open volatility and close to close volatility. In Kola Lumpur, it was high in 2009- 2010 but in Korea and Taiwan it was very high in 2000 – 2001. These countries were not affected by the global financial crisis.

Korean stock market is also very stable from the standard deviation angle. But this market has also not much appreciated over these years and it remains more or less range- bound. Hong Kong has shown the highest volatility as it is a much traded stock exchange. It is more volatile than the other stock exchanges. The volatility has remained more or less constant over the years. The volatility of the Indian Stock Exchange has risen steadily over these years as the trading and market capitalization of the companies has increased. Now the volatility of NSE is almost at par with the other exchanges.

In the developed countries the volatility was very high in the year 2008 – 2009 but in US the inter-day volatility was very high in 2000 – 2001. The period 2001-03 faced another major economic dampener in the form of the 9/11 attacks in USA. This left the world economy in a state of shock. In France it was very high in 2002 – 2003. The financial turmoil affected the markets in India also and India faced an unprecedented withdrawal of FIIs which created a huge hole in the foreign exchange market that resulted in sinking of the rupee to a new low against the dollar. The Reserve Bank of India had to spend $63 billion of its reserves to prop up the rupee. It also cut the Cash Reserve Ratio and repo rates twice that released Rs185,000 crore in the financial system. But banks have remained cautious not lending even to prime borrowers because they fear defaults in the global recessionary situation.

Table 5.13: Stock Index Daily High-Low and Open -Close Volatility (percentage (Emerging Countries China, Indonesia and Kola Lumpur)

Year	*China*		*Indonesia*		*Kola Lumpur*	
	High-Low	*Open-Close*	*High-Low*	*Open-Close*	*High-Low*	*Open-Close*
2000-2001	0.783	0.730	1.266	1.178	1.077	1.049
2001-2002	1.219	1.147	1.061	1.005	0.971	0.891
2002-2003	0.975	0.912	1.135	1.021	0.651	0.597
2003-2004	0.991	0.917	0.995	0.911	0.629	0.602
2004-2005	1.145	1.072	0.945	0.864	0.583	0.574
2005-2006	1.091	1.052	0.905	0.841	0.418	0.414
2006-2007	1.552	1.464	0.926	0.878	0.638	0.625
2007-2008	1.958	1.904	1.108	1.056	0.828	0.792
2008-2009	2.241	2.138	1.593	1.114	0.844	0.805
2009-2010	1.430	1.361	1.281	1.210	0.627	0.572
2010 -2011	1.201	1.143	1.114	1.023	0.441	0.421
2011- 2012	–	0.776	1.163	1.064	0.582	0.592
2000–2012	–	–	1.140	1.054	0.751	0.684

Table 5.14: Stock Index Daily High - Low and Open -Close Volatility (percentage) (Emerging Countries Korea, India and Taiwan)

Year	*Korea*		*India*		*Taiwan*	
	High-Low	*Open-Close*	*High-Low*	*Open-Close*	*High-Low*	*Open-Close*
2000-2001	2.009	1.958	1.901	1.871	1.646	1.518
2001-2002	1.369	1.311	1.370	1.362	1.465	1.361
2002-2003	1.463	1.385	0.941	0.920	1.267	1.177
2003-2004	1.059	1.039	1.380	1.362	0.936	0.882
2004-2005	1.174	1.132	1.512	1.416	0.959	0.901
2005-2006	0.915	0.897	1.019	1.007	0.652	0.611
2006-2007	0.794	0.771	1.701	1.672	0.721	0.678
2007-2008	1.176	1.155	1.914	1.875	1.003	0.957
2008-2009	1.991	1.979	2.413	2.317	1.383	1.264
2009-2010	1.012	1.001	1.640	1.542	1.066	1.012
2010 -2011	0.768	0.742	0.990	0.954	0.686	0.651
2011- 2012	1.096	1.073	1.060	1.042	0.869	0.824
2000–2012	1.295	1.256	1.548	1.506	1.067	0.996

Table 5.15: Stock Index Daily High-Low and Open -Close Volatility (percentage) (Developed Countries Australia, Singapore and Japan)

Year	*Australia*		*Singapore*		*Japan*	
	High-Low	*Open-Close*	*High-Low*	*Open-Close*	*High-Low*	*Open-Close*
2000-2001	0.653	0.583	1.062	0.989	1.271	1.214
2001-2002	0.629	0.559	1.005	0.955	1.299	1.218
2002-2003	0.601	0.522	0.873	0.811	1.134	1.102
2003-2004	0.391	0.370	0.815	0.793	0.998	0.971
2004-2005	0.339	0.315	0.561	0.541	0.743	0.706
2005-2006	0.460	0.414	0.493	0.479	0.751	0.695
2006-2007	0.563	0.483	0.656	0.641	0.817	0.791
2007-2008	0.966	0.854	1.045	1.012	0.995	0.930
2008-2009	1.396	1.295	1.879	1.745	1.856	1.626
2009-2010	0.781	0.714	1.139	1.052	0.884	0.846
2010 -2011	0.797	0.803	0.698	0.645	0.970	0.925
2011- 2012	0.817	0.735	0.920	0.823	0.657	0.651
2000–2012	0.752	0.687	0.993	0.929	1.081	1.010

Since the sub-prime crisis began, Indian exports have been affected by lower demand of American consumers and there has been a fall in the export growth by 15 per cent and more recently, by another 12 per cent. Most affected have been the software firms which had extensive business relations with the American financial

Table 5.16: Stock Index Daily High-Low and Open - Close Volatility (percentage) Developed Countries France, Germany, Hong-Kong US and UK)

Year	*France*		*Germany*		*Hong-Kong*		*US*		*UK*	
	High-Low	*Open-Close*	*High-Low*	*Open-Close*	*High-Low*	*Open-Close*	*High-Low*	*Open-Close*	*High-Low*	*Open-Close*
2000-2001	1.314	1.276	1.231	1.197	1.277	1.249	3.152	2.960	1.040	0.985
2001-2002	1.643	1.632	1.341	1.328	1.124	1.091	2.311	2.247	1.160	1.135
2002-2003	2.513	2.429	1.946	1.847	0.807	0.772	2.084	1.989	1.677	1.579
2003-2004	1.342	1.305	1.007	1.013	0.805	0.793	2.406	1.086	0.779	0.743
2004-2005	0.744	0.716	0.604	0.593	0.737	0.736	0.911	0.874	0.535	0.509
2005-2006	0.623	0.609	0.545	0.539	0.531	0.522	0.745	0.731	0.524	0.497
2006-2007	0.784	0.760	0.723	0.705	0.679	0.642	0.882	0.877	0.721	0.666
2007-2008	1.062	1.027	1.074	1.021	1.318	1.312	1.026	1.093	1.166	1.079
2008-2009	2.062	2.029	1.908	1.904	1.981	1.869	2.176	2.094	2.036	1.871
2009-2010	1.165	1.123	1.238	1.201	1.134	1.102	1.007	1.012	1.072	1.043
2010 -2011	1.162	1.152	0.977	0.982	0.741	0.734	1.041	1.063	0.991	0.942
2011- 2012	1.460	1.430	1.555	1.552	0.941	0.941	1.057	1.052	1.213	1.163
2000–2012	1.256	1.228	1.427	1.394	1.075	1.043	1.645	1.576	1.157	1.091

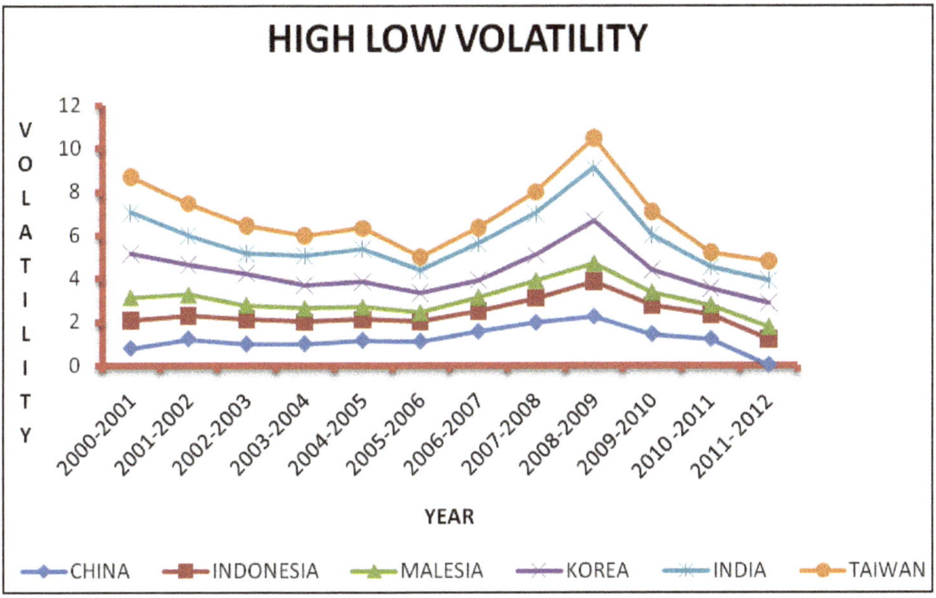

Figure 5.21: High Low Volatility for Developing Countries (2000 – 2012).

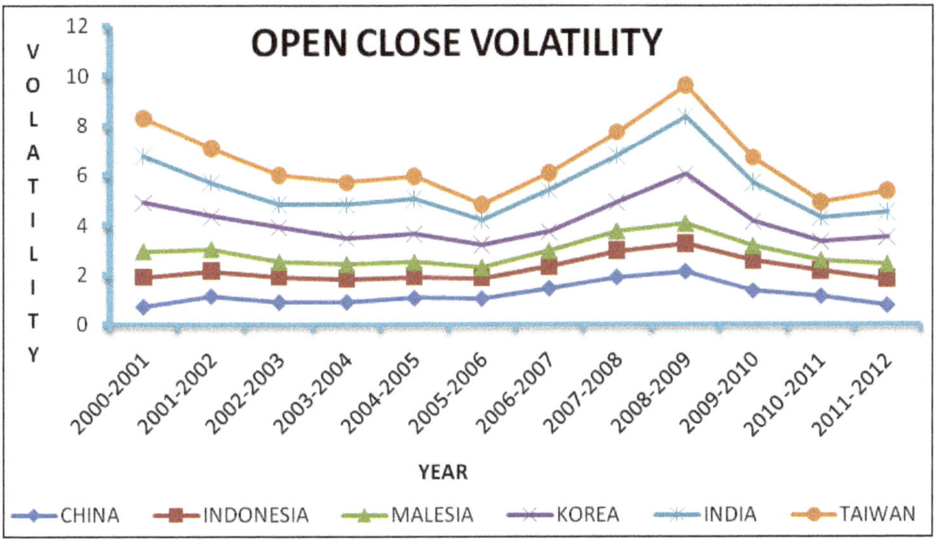

Figure 5.22: Open Close Volatility for Developing Countries (2000 – 2012).

sector and are now faced with low demand. President Elect Barack Obama has not been encouraging about outsourcing as he is concerned about jobs remaining in US. India's labour intensive industries like diamond, carpets, textiles and garments, have all been facing job cuts and mass retrenchment. The real estate sector and cement production are also in trouble because of liquidity problems.

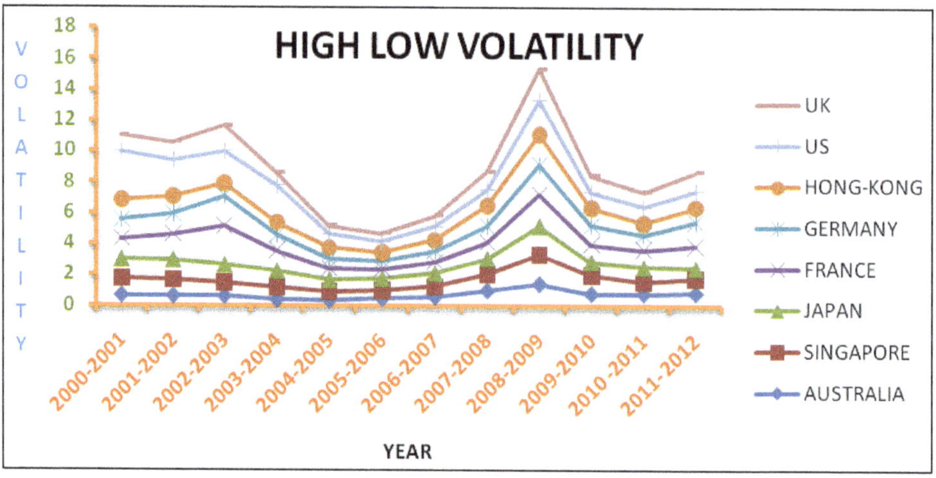

Figure 5.23: High Low Volatility for Developed Countries (2000 – 2012).

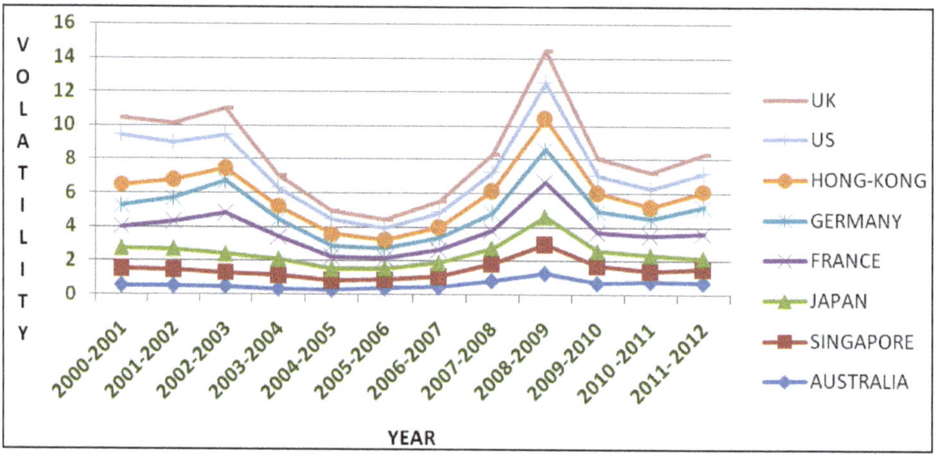

Figure 5.24: Open Close Volatility for Developed Countries (2000 – 2012).

It appears that the US scores over other developed markets in terms of intra-day volatility. In the UK, open to open volatility is slightly higher than high-low volatility and open to close volatilities. The volatility is on the rise for the past three year's *i.e.* from 2006 -2007 to 2008-2009. USA scored higher volatility compared to all the developed markets. The open - close volatility, in case of France, is lower than open to open and close to close volatility. In the year 2008-09, in France UK and USA it almost touched 2 percentage points and peaked at 2.09 per cent in USA and it appears to be highest among all the developed markets in that year. Intra-day dispersion is also high. Australia appears to have comparatively quieter markets. Intra-day and inter -day movements in stock prices are considerably stable in Australia. Intra -day volatility has been consistently lower than 1 per cent except 2008 – 2009 and even the high and low price movement variation is also low.

Emerging markets exhibited higher intra-day volatility compared to developed markets. Owing to economic and socio-political variations, the volatility in the emerging markets was generally on the high side. Among all the emerging countries studied, India experienced very high intra-day volatility followed by Indonesia, South Korea, Taiwan, Kola Lumpur and China. From the year 2004-05 to 2008-09 the volatility was very high in China and India. Among all the emerging markets the intra-day volatility was very high in India and China in the year 2008-09. Except USA all the developed countries volatility was at its peak in the year 2008-09. In the first quarter of 2008 the market slumped following bad news from the global markets. The world stock markets suffered loss in this quarter. The loss as well as the volatility was very high in the Indian stock market. The fifth largest US investment bank Bear Stearns' liquidity position deteriorated significantly, and the Federal Reserve's emergency cut in its discount rate created setback in the stock markets. Benchmarks (Sensex) cracked following a sharp setback in global markets, selling by foreign institutional investors. On 22nd January 2008 market wide circuit filters were applied after key benchmark indices fell by 10 per cent within minutes of commencement of trade. The four year boom ended on 21 January 2008. Indian shares were heavily affected by the sell-off on 21 January, Monday. Financial stocks fell sharply, with the ICICI Bank losing 10 per cent and the State Bank of India, the nation's largest, dropping 5.6 per cent. Overseas funds sold $691 million of Indian stocks. India is also being hit by inflation. Prices of wheat, aluminum, steel and other items had gone up sharply. As a result, investors were taking less interest in stocks and finding safer investment in gold, minerals and oil and the rupee was falling against the US dollar in 2008. In respect of volatility, the Indian market moved in tandem with the US stock market with a slight difference. The volatility registered a significant jump the last quarter, rising by more than 100 per cent. These figures suggest that the risk reward structure of the Indian stock market has noticeably weakened in the post – financial crisis period. The global financial crisis has affected the market performance in the long run, making it more volatile and more prone to spillovers from foreign markets. The extreme volatility of the Indian stock exchange in the recent periods may find its root in the internal as well as the global factors. Close to close and open to open volatility moved in tandem with little divergence in a few periods.

5.4 Conclusion

The descriptive statistics were used to know the properties of the series. Among all the markets Indonesia earned highest income (0.0680) and India earned (0.0413) in the long run. Emerging markets performed better than developed markets. Except Taiwan all the emerging markets earned return in the long run. Indonesia and India performed better than the rest of the emerging markets and many of the major markets. Among developed markets Australia Singapore and Hong Kong all the other markets suffered loss in the long run. In India, open to open and close to close volatility appears to be neck to neck. In the developed countries except Australia interlay volatility was very low in the year 2005 2006. It clearly exhibits that developed countries moved in tandem with each other. USA scored higher volatility compared to all the developed markets. Intra-day and inter -day movements in stock prices are considerably stable in Australia. Inter -day volatility has been consistently lower than 1 per cent and even the high and low price movement variation is also low. Among all the emerging markets the intra-day volatility was very high in India and China in the year 2008-09. The developed markets UK, Hong-Kong, Singapore; Japan and emerging markets Kola Lumpur, Korea, Taiwan and India moved in tandem.

References

1. Zuliu, H (1995)"Stock market Volatility and Corporate Investment", **IMF Working Paper**, 95/102.
2. Levine, R and S. Zervos (1996)"Stock Market Development and Long-Run Growth", **World, Bank Economic Review**, 10(1):323-339.
3. Arestis, P., P.O. Demetriades and K.B. Luintel (2001)"Financial Development and Economic Growth: The Role of Stock Markets", **Journal of Money, Credit and Banking,** 33(2):16-41.
4. Bekaert, Geert and Campbell, R. Harvey (1995), Emerging Equity MarketVolatility, **National Bureau of Economic Research (NBER), Working Paper 5307**,pages 1 – 77
5. Raju, M.T., Anirban Gosh, "Stock Market Volatility – An International 5Comparisin", **SEBI working Paper Series**, No.8, 2004, p.14.

6-8. **http://www.un.org/en/development/desa/policy/wesp/wesp_archive/wesp2014.pdf**https://www.cia.gov/library/publications/resources/the-world-factbook/Machiko Nissanke (2009), "The Global Financial Crisis and the Developing World: Transmission Channels and Fall-outs for Industrial Development" Research and Statistics Branch Working Paper 06/2009

9. Campbell, J.Y., A.W. Lo, and A.C. Makinlay, **The Econometrics of Financial Markets,** Princeton University Press, Princeton, NJ, 1997.
10. Hardouvelis, G.A. and P.Theodossiou, "The Asymmetric Relation between Initial Margin Requirements and Stock Market Volatility Across Bull and Bear Markets", **Review of Financial Studies**, Vol.15, 2002, pp.1525–1559.
11. India Fights back (2008) http://www.capitalmarket.com/cmedit/story_fight.asp Accessed on January 4, 2009.
12. Asian Economies hit by US Financial crisis and slowdown http://www.wsws.org/articles/2008/mar2008/asec-m20.shtml Accessed on January 8, 2008

Chapter 6

Dynamic Linkages between Indian and other International Stock Markets

6.1 Introduction

Knowledge on stock markets integration is very important for both practitioners and policymakers. Exchanges are now going beyond national boundaries to extend their service areas and this has led to market integration and provide overseas investment options for investors, this encourages the global investors to look for investment opportunities internationally to diversify their portfolios and to reduce their portfolio's risk and improve the image of the exchange for investors and attracts more volume. Financial resources are scarce in developing countries they are in need of external sources to strengthen their economy. Foreign capital investment fills the resource gap of developing countries. Financial integration leads to rapid flow of funds from 'less returns markets' to 'high returns markets' and in this process it brings about equality in returns. Financing and investing decisions by individuals, corporate and particularly multinationals are greatly influenced by the perceived degree of market integration. Foreign capital can be easily generated through market integration but these markets are vulnerable for the financial crises that are happening in other regions. The global financial crisis had affected the stock markets. It is very interesting to examine whether the financial crisis has affected the long term and short term relationship between Indian and other developing and developed markets.

Liberalization of Financial Markets accelerated Financial Market integration. An open and well-integrated financial market helps to maximize the benefits of an increasing globalised economy. A financial market that is well integrated with the rest of the world allows country to smooth its consumption pattern and attract investment from abroad to enhance its productivity. Integration of financial markets helps developing nations in achieving high economic growth and improve living standard by opening international pool of resources. It also adds depth and liquidity to the domestic capital markets and permits it to perform its intermediation and risk diversification roles more efficiently. Highly integrated financial markets also help individuals and investors to diversify their portfolio risk by investing in different countries worldwide.

If stock markets move together then investing in various markets would not generate any long term gain to portfolio diversification; and if these markets are independent, investors in these countries can invest in different markets of the region to diversify their portfolio.The authorities in the region need not worry about any contagious effects if one market experiences any turmoil. The existence of international portfolio diversification was carried out by Grubel, (1968), who expounded the benefits of international portfolio diversification. Hence, understanding the behaviour of the inter linkage among markets is essential for international financial management, especially in the context of international portfolio diversification and hedging.

6.2 Cointegration among Indian and Developing and Developed Stock Markets

When markets are integrated then a shock arising in one market gets quickly transmitted to other interrelated markets. In general two time series are cointegrated when a linear combination of the time series is stationary, even though each series may individually be nonstationary. Since nonstationary time series do not return to their long-run average values following a disturbance, it is important to convert them to stationary process; otherwise regressing one nonstationary process on other nonstationary process can generate spurious results. If a time series contains a stochastic trend, it is said to be integrated of order 'd' that is I (d), and differencing the series d times yields a stationary series. Since market index series are likely to be I (1) process they will tend to be nonstationary at levels but stationary in first differences.

If the stock prices in countries i and j are cointegrated, stock price changes in country i (country j) are predictable. If the stock prices in countries i and j are determined independently, then stock prices in country i (country j) incorporate all available information. Hence, from the past stock prices in country i (country j), no other information will be useful to explain changes in its stock prices.

Asim Gosh (1999)[1], Golaka C. Nath (2002)[2], Jian Yang (2002)[3], Ali F. Darrat and Omar M. Benkato (2003)[4], Tatsuyoshi Miyakoshi (2003)[5], Asjeet Lamba (2004)[6], Hsiao, Cheng *et al.* (2005)[7], Kuper and Lestano (2006)[9], Dimitris Kenourgious *et al.* (2007)[10], Siew-yen at el (2008)[11], Bhar and Nikolova (2009)[12], Saleem (2009)[13], Huyghebaert and Wang (2010)[14], Claus and Lucey (2012)[15] made an attempt to trace the interrelationship among stock markets.

Several researchers have examined the short-and long-run relationships among the major developed equity markets and markets in the Asian region. Kate Phylakktis and Fabiola Ravazzolo(1998)[16], Asim Gosh (1999)[17], Jian Yang (2002)[18], Golaka C. Nath (2002)[19] studied the inter-linkage among the markets and showed the non-existence of any such relationship with a few exceptions such as Taiwan and Thailand did not appear to be influenced by the stock markets of the US or Japan.

In order to test whether the two market indices are cointegrated, it is necessary to first determine that each index series is stationary. If they are nonstationary, the index series are then examined to determine whether they are cointegrated.

6.2.1 Augmented Dickey–Fuller Test

Augmented Dickey Fuller test examines the presence of unit root in the time series. Augmented Dickey–Fuller test is used on the market index levels and their first differences to test for unit root in the data. To perform the ADF test, for each market index series, the following regression is estimated.

$$\Delta Y_t = \beta_1 + \beta_2 t + \delta Y_{t-1} + \alpha_i \sum_{i=1}^{m} \Delta Y_{t-i} + \mu_t \qquad (1)$$

Where μ_t is a white noise error term and $\Delta Y_{t-1} = (Y_{t-1} - Y_{t-2})$. $Y_t = \text{Ln}(Y_t)$. ADF still test whether $\delta = 0$

The null and alternative hypotheses are

$H_0: \ \delta = 0$

$H_1: \ \delta \neq 0$

The acceptance of the null hypothesis implies nonstationarity. The critical value of ADF test at five per cent level of significance is –3.41. The ADF test and Philip Peron values on the stock returns are given in Table 6.1

The calculated tau (τ) values of δ and Philip Peron values for all the stock market indices return are more than the tabulated value. These values are significant at 1 per cent level. The ADF test and Philip Peron results prove that all the stock market indices are stationary at market index returns. All the series are stationary for the entire sample period and the sub – sample periods.

6.2.2 Engle–Granger ADF Test

Correlation analysis helps in determining the degree of relationship between two or more variables. An increase in correlation is often taken as evidence of an increase in the degree of market integration and a higher tendency that shock in one country is transmitted to another. However, such an approach is not the most informative one since correlations are determined by short-term trading noises as well as by long term fundamental relationship among the markets. Short-term variations in prices can obscure the image of the long-run relationship among the markets induced by the growing liberalization. To solve this problem, it is useful to look at the long-run relationship among international financial markets based on the idea of cointegration introduced by Engle and Granger (1987).

Table 6.1: Unit Root Tests on Returns

Countries	*Augmented Dickey Fuller*			*Philip Peron*		
	(2000–2007)	*2007-2012*	*2000–2012*	*(2000–2007)*	*2007-2012*	*2000–2012*
China	–41.608*	–34.030*	–53.845*	–41.617*	–34.030*	–53.845*
Indonesia	–37.345*	–30.436*	–42.556*	–37.348*	–30.297*	–42.489*
KolaLumpur	–34.379*	–45.657*	–60.685*	–34.294*	–45.814*	–60.514*
Korea	–41.775*	–33.502*	–51.278*	–41.668*	–33.514*	–51.323*
India	–38.128*	–32.330*	–50.445*	–37.981*	32.293*	–50.445*
Taiwan	–40.668*	–35.312*	–53.942*	–40.690*	–32.329*	–53.907*
Australia	–45.314*	–38.614*	–51.653*	–45.275*	–38.690*	–51.652*
Singapore	–41.412*	–34.786*	–54.368*	–41.412*	–34.788*	–54.407*
Japan	–42.858*	–35.493*	–55.859*	–42.862*	–35.735*	–56.065*
France	–44.105*	–36.367*	–57.244*	–44.713*	–36.954*	–57.792*
Germany	–44.554*	–34.725*	–56.354*	–44.604*	–34.778*	–56.382*
Hong Kong	–42.040*	–36.093*	–56.205*	–42.040*	–36.193*	–56.205*
US	–44.694*	–38.602*	–58.668*	–45.031*	–38.793*	–59.358*
UK	–45.066*	–36.218*	–57.760*	–45.726*	–36.770*	–57.994*

The critical value for ADF test at 5 per cent level of significance is -3.41.

* Significant at 1 per cent level.

According to Engle and Granger (1987), if two random walks price series have a long-run equilibrium relationship, they cannot drift apart indefinitely. The deviation from their long-run equilibrium relationship must be stationary with zero mean. In this case, the two price series are said to be cointegrated. This idea can be extended into a multivariate setting. If there is really a long-run equilibrium relationship among non-stationary price series, then there is a combination of the non-stationary price series which is stationary

In the first step the cointegrating coefficient δ is estimated by ordinary least squares with the following formula:

$$X_t = \beta_1 + \delta Y_t + \mu_t \tag{2}$$

This regression is called cointegrating regression. Then the Engle-Granger ADF test is conducted on 'cointegrating residuals', obtained from the cointegrating regression by using the following equation.

The Engle Granger Augmented Dickey–Fuller test is applied on the 'co integrtating residuals' μ_t received from the equation 1. The formula for EG–ADF test is as follows

$$\Delta\mu_t = -\delta\mu_{t-1} + a_i \sum_{i=1}^{m} \Delta\mu_{t-1} + \mu_t \tag{3}$$

Where $\Delta\mu_t$ represents the first difference of the error term.

This two step procedure is called the Engle–Granger DF test for cointegration or EG–DF (Engle–Granger 1987)

The specific hypotheses are:

H_0: $\delta = 0$

H_1: $\delta \neq 0$

Null hypothesis is that there is no co integration among the stock indices. The value of a calculated absolute tau (τ) value is greater than the tabulated critical (τ) value; the null hypothesis of no cointegration is rejected. Engle and Granger have provided the critical values of ADF statistics. The results of EG–ADF test are given in Tables 6.2–6.4 for pre-crisis period, post-crisis period and the whole period respectively.

Table 6.2: Engle-Granger ADF Test of Cointegration (2000–2007) (Lag 5)

Name of the Indices	δ	*Probability*
India on China	–0.124	0.983
China on India	0.369	0.995
India on Indonesia	–3.017	0.106
Indonesia on India	–2.976	0.116
India on Kolalumpur	–2.701	0.199
Kolalumpur on India	–2.606	0.235
India on Korea	–2.364	0.342
Korea on India	–2.418	0.316
India on Taiwan	–2.836	0.155
Taiwan on India	–4.046**	0.006
India on Australia	–2.641	0.261
Australia on India	–2.500	0.327
India on Singapore	–2.323	0.361
Singapore on India	–2.247	0.399
India on Japan	–1.981	0.538
Japan on India	–3.233	0.065
India on France	–0.085	0.984
France on India	–1.705	0.675
India on Germany	–0.475	0.984
Germany on India	–1.665	0.766
India on Hong-Kong	–1.852	0.604
Hong –Kong on India	–2.084	0.484
India on US	0.455	0.996
US on India	–3.029	0.103
India on UK	–0.504	0.962
UK on India	–1.799	0.630

** Significant at 1 per cent level MacKinnon (1996) p-values.

Table 6.3: Engle-Granger ADF Test of Cointegration (2007–2012) (Lag 5)

Name of the Indices	δ	*Probability*
India on China	–1.604	0.720
China on India	–1.391	0.802
India on Indonesia	–1.988	0.534
Indonesia on India	–1.381	0.805
India on Kolalumpur	–2.858	0.148
Kolalumpur on India	–2.501	0.279
India on Korea	3.210	0.082
Korea on India	3.174	0.090
India on Taiwan	–3.371	0.046*
Taiwan on India	–3.441	0.038*
India on Australia	–1.827	0.616
Australia on India	–2.439	0.306
India on Singapore	–3.369	0.046*
Singapore on India	–3.571	0.027*
India on Japan	–1.557	0.740
Japan on India	–2.918	0.131
India on France	–1.589	0.727
France on India	–2.596	0.239
India on Germany	–2.526	0.314
Germany on India	–2.721	0.228
India on Hong-Kong	–2.149	0.450
Hong –Kong on India	–2.337	0.355
India on US	–1.927	0.566
US on India	–1.340	0.819
India on UK	–2.838	0.154
UK on India	–3.252	0.062

*Significant at 5 per cent level.

Before the financial crisis India influenced Taiwan. There was no long run relationship between India and other countries during the pre crisis period. All the calculated values are less than the tabulated tau (τ) vale. That is $\delta = 0$. The null hypothesis, that there is no cointegration is accepted.

But after global financial crisis there was a long run relationship between India and Taiwan and India and Singapore. It ensured that the price movements of India Taiwan and Singapore are not independent. During the whole study period there is a long run relationship between India and Taiwan, India and Korea. Indian stock market influenced US stock market and Kola Lumpur stock market influenced India. All other countries can enjoy benefits of the diversification.

Table 6.4: Engle-Granger ADF Test of Cointegration (2000–2012) (Lag 5)

Name of the Indices	δ	*Probability*
India on China	–1.044	0.936
China on India	–1.492	0.832
India on Indonesia	–3.159	0.092
Indonesia on India	–3.060	0.116
India on Kolalumpur	–3.471	0.042*
Kolalumpur on India	–3.332	0.061
India on Korea	–3.687	0.023*
Korea on India	–3.716	0.021*
India on Taiwan	–3.670	0.024*
Taiwan on India	–4.321	0.002**
India on Australia	–1.172	0.914
Australia on India	–1.719	0.742
India on Singapore	–2.532	0.312
Singapore on India	–2.692	0.239
India on Japan	–0.516	0.982
Japan on India	–2.646	0.259
India on France	–0.604	0.978
France on India	–1.992	0.604
India on Germany	–2.014	0.5928
Germany on India	–2.628	0.267
India on Hong-Kong	–2.962	0.143
Hong –Kong on India	–3.184	0.087
India on US	–1.698	0.752
US on India	–3.535	0.035*
India on UK	–1.365	0.870
UK on India	–2.524	0.315

* ** Significant at 5 per cent level and 1 per cent level.

6.2.3 Granger Causality Test

Granger Theorem is based on the principal that if two variables are co-integrated, there must be a causal relationship between them at least in one direction. Co-integration investigates the existence of long run relationship but does not explain the lead lag relationship which is important in price discovery. Granger Causality is used to determine the lead lag relationship. If the leading series is determined, the other lag series can be predicted. Causality in one direction is known as unidirectional causality which means the flow of information from one market to another market. If the existence of lead lag relationship is reported in both directions, it means the flow of information occurs from both sides and both the markets are exerting pressure on each other. This is called bi-directional causality.

The study uses Granger – causality test (1969, 1988) to examine the hypotheses. Formally, a time series x_t Granger – causes another time series y_t if series y_t can be predicted with better accuracy by using past values of x_t rather than by not doing so, other information being identical. In other words, variable x_t fails Granger –cause y_t if

$$\Pr(y_{t+m} \mid \Omega_t) = \Pr(y_{t+m} \mid \Psi_t) \tag{4}$$

Where $\Pr(y_{t+m} \mid \Omega_t)$ denotes conditional probability of y_t, Ω_t is the set of all information available at time t, and $\Pr(y_{t+m} \mid \Psi_t)$ denotes conditional probability of y_t obtained by excluding all information on x_t from y_t this set of information is depicted as Ψ_t.

The hypotheses are tested in the context of VAR of the following form:

$$x_t = \alpha_0 + \sum_{j=1}^{k} \gamma_j + x_{t-j} + \sum_{j=1}^{k} \beta_j y_{t-j} + \mu_{xy} \tag{5}$$

$$y_t = \alpha_0 + \sum_{j=1}^{k} \gamma_j + x_{t-j} + \sum_{j=1}^{k} \beta_j y_{t-j} + \mu_{xy} \tag{6}$$

Where k is a suitably chosen positive integer, γ_j and β_j, j = 0,1 ......k are parameters and α' are constants; and μ_t's are disturbance terms with zero means and finite variances. The null hypothesis that y_t does not Granger – cause x_t is not accepted if the β_j's, j>0 in equation (5) are jointly significantly different from zero using a standard joint test (*e.g.*, and F test). Similarly, x_t Granger – causes y_t, if the γ_j's j >0 coefficients in equation (6) are jointly different from zero.

To test the hypotheses, the restricted F-test is applied, which is given by:

$$F = [(RSS_r - RSSU_r)/m] / [RSSU_r/(n-k)] \tag{7}$$

Where, m is number of lagged terms and k is the number of parameters and RSS_R and RSS_{UR} are residual sum of squares of restricted and unrestricted models respectively. Granger causality test captures lead lag relationship within the sample period. The Results of Granger Causality are given in Table 6.5–6.7.

During the pre crisis period there was a unidirectional Granger causality running from India to Indonesia, Kola Lumpur, Taiwan, Japan, Hong Kong and Germany. Bidirectional Granger causality exists between India and Korea, Australia and Singapore. During the post crisis period there was a unidirectional Granger causality running from India to China, Kola Lumpur, Korea, Taiwan, Australia, Japan and Hong Kong and unidirectional Granger causality running from Singapore, France, and US to India. Bidirectional Granger causality exists between India and Indonesia, India and Germany and India and UK during the post crisis period.

6.2.4 Cross Correlation

The stationary series are also cross – correlated. The cross - correlation between the time series are tested by using the following formula:

Table 6.5: Granger Causality Test Results

Pre-Crisis Period (April 2000 - June 2007) F-statistic		
	F-Statistic	*Causality Inference*
INDIA→CHINA	4.43	0.001
CHINA→INDIA	1.17	0.318
INDIA→INDONESIA	2.91	0.020*
INDONESIA→INDIA	1.58	0.176
INDIA → KOLALUMPUR	6.12	0.000**
KOLALUMPUR→INDIA	0.06	0.991
INDIA → KOREA	4.21	0.002**
KOREA → INDIA	4.85	0.000**
INDIA→TAIWAN	11.32	0.000**
TAIWAN→INDIA	1.34	0.251
INDIA → AUSTRALIA	5.80	0.000**
AUSTRALIA → INDIA	3.93	0.003**
INDIA → SINGAPORE	5.43	0.000**
SINGAPORE→ INDIA	2.48	0.0421*
INDIA → JAPAN	9.67	0.000**
JAPAN → INDIA	1.69	0.148
INDIA → FRANCE	1.51	0.194
FRANCE → INDIA	10.79	0.000
INDIA → GERMANY	2.66	0.030*
GERMANY → INDIA	13.35	0.000
INDIA → HONGKONG	4.45	0.001**
HONGKONG → INDIA	6.57	0.000
INDIA → US	1.01	0.399
US → INDIA	16.58	0.0000
INDIA → UK	1.35	0.248
UK → INDIA	8.36	0.000

* Significant at 1 per cent level.

Table 6.6: Granger Causality Test Results

	Post Crisis Period (July 2007 - April 2012) F-statistic	
	F-Statistic	*Causality Inference*
INDIA→CHINA	3.52	0.007**
CHINA→INDIA	1.50	0.198
INDIA→INDONESIA	5.05	0.000**
INDONESIA→INDIA	15.67	0.000**
INDIA → KOLALUMPUR	26.67	0.000**
KOLALUMPUR→INDIA	0.89	0.466
INDIA → KOREA	15.42	0.000**
KOREA → INDIA	2.04	0.085
INDIA→TAIWAN	15.65	0.000**
TAIWAN→INDIA	1.56	0.180
INDIA → AUSTRALIA	15.18	0.000**
AUSTRALIA → INDIA	0.59	0.723
INDIA → SINGAPORE	1.66	0.156
SINGAPORE→ INDIA	4.23	0.002**
INDIA → JAPAN	17.39	0.000**
JAPAN → INDIA	1.21	0.301
INDIA → FRANCE	2.22	0.064
FRANCE → INDIA	6.33	0.000**
INDIA → GERMANY	7.22	0.000**
GERMANY → INDIA	3.48	0.007**
INDIA → HONGKONG	9.86	0.000**
HONGKONG → INDIA	0.38	0.820
INDIA → US	0.98	0.415
US → INDIA	27.29	0.000**
INDIA → UK	2.98	0.017*
UK → INDIA	7.64	0.000**

* Significant at 1 per cent level.

Table 6.7: Granger Causality Test Results

Full Sample Period April 2000 - December 2012 F-statistic		
	F-Statistic	*Causality Inference*
INDIA→CHINA	4.09	0.002**
CHINA→INDIA	0.727	0.573
INDIA→INDONESIA	7.64	0.000**
INDONESIA→INDIA	9.74	0.000**
INDIA → KOLALUMPUR	24.19	0.000**
KOLALUMPUR→INDIA	0.33	0.854
INDIA → KOREA	16.23	0.000**
KOREA → INDIA	5.19	0.000**
INDIA→TAIWAN	25.25	0.000**
TAIWAN→INDIA	0.702	0.589
INDIA → AUSTRALIA	21.13	0.000**
AUSTRALIA → INDIA	0.95	0.430
INDIA → SINGAPORE	3.74	0.004**
SINGAPORE→ INDIA	4.32	0.001**
INDIA → JAPAN	23.14	0.000**
JAPAN → INDIA	2.40	0.047*
INDIA → FRANCE	1.35	0.2470
FRANCE → INDIA	15.82	0.000**
INDIA → GERMANY	6.82	0.000**
GERMANY → INDIA	15.22	0.000**
INDIA → HONGKONG	14.13	0.000*
HONGKONG → INDIA	4.82	0.000**
INDIA → US	3.77	0.004**
US → INDIA	1.98	0.094
INDIA → UK	1.94	0.099
UK → INDIA	15.73	0.000**

* Significant at 5 per cent level.

$$\gamma_{x_y\ y_t}(k) = \frac{\sum_{t=1}^{T-K}(x_t - \bar{x})(y_{t+k} - \bar{y})}{\left[\sum_{t=1}^{T}(x_t - \bar{x})^2 \sum_{t=1}^{T}(y_t - \bar{y})^2\right]^{1/2}} \tag{8}$$

Where k is greater than, equal to, or less than zero.

The significance of estimated cross – correlation is assessed by using approximate standard error, $T^{-1/2}$, (Bartlet, 1966), of the sample of cross – correlation. This helps to identify the causality patterns associated with, $\gamma x_t\ y_t(k)$. This method was used, among others, by Ahmad (1989) in estimating the cross – correlations between two interest rate series. The results of Cross- Correlation are given in Tables 6.8–6.16.

Table 6.8: Cross-correlations on Daily Returns (2000–2007)

Lags	*India-China*	*India-Inodnesia*	*India-Kola Lumpur*	*India-Korea*	*India-Taiwan*
–5	–0.018	0.044	0.033	0.020	0.008
–4	0.043	0.023	0.031	0.018	0.011
–3	–0.0186	–0.021	–0.008	0.025	0.018
–2	–0.000	–0.031	–0.008	0.022	0.009
–1	0.023	0.010	0.010	0.104*	0.017
0	0.053*	0.324*	0.186*	0.324*	0.278*
1	0.039	0.089*	0.101*	0.074*	0.142*
2	0.004	0.022	0.008	0.005	0.039
3	–0.020	0.030	0.043	0.030	0.008
4	–0.001	0.049*	0.024	–0.000	0.018
5	0.022	0.060*	0.008	0.002	0.040

* Significant at 1 per cent level.

Table 6.9: Cross-correlations on Daily Returns (2000–2007)

Lags	*India-Singapore*	*India-Australia*	*India-Japan*	*India-France*
–5	–0.002	0.018	0.024	–0.007
–4	0.046	–0.010	0.026	–0.002
–3	0.029	0.012	0.017	0.066*
–2	0.027	0.057*	0.011	0.023
–1	0.064*	0.034	0.047	0.137*
0	0.387*	0.334*	0.314*	0.202

Contd...

Table 6.9–*Contd...*

Lags	*India-Singapore*	*India-Australia*	*India-Japan*	*India-France*
1	0.088*	0.089*	0.090*	0.003
2	0.010	–0.020	–0.026	–0.021
3	0.029	0.014	0.046	0.007
4	0.065*	0.027	0.039	0.017
5	0.013	–0.003	–0.006	–0.008

* Significant at 1 per cent level.

Table 6.10: Cross-correlations on Daily Returns (2000–2007)

Lags	*India-Germany*	*India-Hong Kong*	*India-US*	*India-UK*
–5	–0.022	–0.014	0.002	0.014
–4	0.026	0.055*	0.028	0.005
–3	0.027	0.045	0.066*	0.037
–2	0.024	0.070*	0.018	0.0412
–1	0.014	0.033	0.169*	0.129*
0	0.182*	0.370*	0.108*	0.223*
1	0.158*	0.066*	0.008	–0.014
2	0.030	–0.000	0.001	–0.017
3	0.060*	0.030	0.006	0.000
4	–0.017	0.028	0.016	0.018
5	0.007	0.008	–0.028	–0.022

* Significant at 1 per cent level.

Table 6.11: Cross-correlations on Daily Returns (2007–2012)

Lags	*India-China*	*India-Inodnesia*	*India-Kola Lumpur*	*India-Korea*	*India-Taiwan*
–5	–0.055	–0.044	0.008	–0.008	–0.006
–4	–0.052	–0.045	0.007	–0.019	–0.034
–3	0.031	0.027	–0.008	–0.026	0.007
–2	0.007	0.200*	–0.047	–0.034	–0.003
–1	–0.040	0.066*	0.032	0.085*	0.051
0	0.326*	0.383*	0.259*	0.462*	0.441*
1	0.094*	0.148*	0.155*	0.201*	0.221*
2	–0.023	0.033	0.020	0.017	0.016
3	0.054	0.011	0.043	0.004	0.028
4	0.039	0.013	–0.004	–0.012	–0.039
5	0.023	–0.013	0.030	0.022	–0.014

* Significant at 1 per cent level.

Table 6.12: Cross-correlations on Daily Returns (2007–2012)

Lags	*India-Singapore*	*India-Australia*	*India-Japan*	*India-France*
–5	0.007	0.004	–0.009	–0.016
–4	–0.076*	–0.017	–0.064*	–0.034
–3	0.025	–0.005	0.000	0.015
–2	–0.014	–0.028	0.042	0.032
–1	0.073*	0.057*	0.031	0.137*
0	0.664*	0.469*	0.423*	0.452*
1	0.041	0.192*	0.202*	0.035
2	0.020	0.008	–0.076*	–0.030
3	0.007	–0.005	–0.018	–0.029
4	–0.006	–0.026	–0.005	–0.003
5	–0.009	–0.038	–0.064*	–0.039

* Significant at 1 per cent level.

Table 6.13: Cross-correlations on Daily Returns (2007–2012)

Lags	*India-Germany*	*India-Hong Kong*	*India-US*	*India-UK*
–5	0.012	–0.061*	–0.016	–0.036
–4	0.004	–0.059	–0.014	–0.017
–3	0.031	0.011	0.019	0.036
–2	0.020	–0.001	–0.029	0.026
–1	0.101	0.047	0.042	0.141*
0	0.392	0.644*	–0.008	0.461*
1	0.116	0.136	–0.010	0.037
2	–0.021	–0.043	0.035	–0.038
3	0.031	0.004	0.014	–0.050
4	–0.011	–0.060*	–0.001	0.013
5	–0.021	–0.012	–0.005	–0.034

* Significant at 1 per cent level.

Table 6.14: Cross-correlations on Daily Returns (2000–2012)

Lags	*India-China*	*India-Inodnesia*	*India-Kola Lumpur*	*India-Korea*	*India-Taiwan*
–5	–0.037*	–0.001	0.019	0.008	0.002
–4	–0.007	–0.012	0.017	0.002	–0.009
–3	0.007	0.003	–0.008	0.002	0.013
–2	0.004	0.088*	–0.030	–0.003	0.003
–1	–0.010	0.039*	0.023	0.095*	0.033

Contd...

Table 6.14–*Contd...*

Lags	*India-China*	*India-Inodnesia*	*India-Kola Lumpur*	*India-Korea*	*India-Taiwan*
0	0.199*	0.355*	0.225*	0.383*	0.352*
1	0.069*	0.120*	0.131*	0.130*	0.178*
2	–0.012	0.028	0.015	0.011	0.028
3	0.019	0.020	0.043	0.019	0.018
4	0.020	0.031	0.008	–0.005	–0.008
5	0.024	0.023	0.021	0.011	0.015

* Significant at 1 per cent level.

Table 6.15: Cross-correlations on Daily Returns (2000–2012)

Lags	*India-Singapore*	*India-Australia*	*India-Japan*	*India-France*
–5	0.002	0.009	–0.012	–0.012
–4	–0.021	–0.014	–0.019	–0.019
–3	0.028	0.002	0.039*	0.039*
–2	0.005	0.004	0.028	0.028
–1	0.069*	0.048	0.137*	0.137*
0	0.539*	0.408*	0.332*	0.332*
1	0.063*	0.150*	0.020	0.020
2	0.016	–0.002	–0.026	–0.026
3	0.017	0.003	–0.011	–0.011
4	0.026	–0.006	0.007	0.007
5	0.001	–0.023	–0.024	–0.024

* Significant at 1 per cent level.

Table 6.16: Cross-correlations on Daily Returns (2000 – 20012)

Lags	*India-Germany*	*India-Hong Kong*	*India-US*	*India-UK*
–5	0.009	–0.041*	–0.011	–0.013
–4	–0.007	–0.010	–0.008	–0.007
–3	0.046*	0.025	0.017	0.037*
–2	0.026	0.029	–0.019	0.033
–1	0.131*	0.041*	0.040*	0.136*
0	0.283*	0.523*	0.001	0.361*
1	0.036	0.105*	–0.007	0.013
2	0.002	–0.025	0.025	–0.029
3	0.029	0.015	0.010	–0.026
4	0.008	–0.022	0.000	0.015
5	–0.022	–0.003	–0.006	–0.029

* Significant at 1 per cent level.

The direction of causality is also checked by using cross – correlations on returns. The results of cross – correlation test are presented in the Table 6.8 to 6.16. The cross – correlation test re- confirm results of Granger – causality test. There is no such significant difference between the markets before and after the financial crisis except Japan. The cross relation between India and Japan is very high after crisis. There is no cross relation between India and Germany and US after the crisis.

The results show evidence of weaker cross correlations among India and European, UK and US stock markets. Hence it can be said that the Indian markets offer diversification benefits to international investors looking for investment in India.

6.5 Conclusion

Cointegration among India and other international stock markets are examined. The traditional test namely cross- correlation and the dynamic test Engle Granger Augmented Dickey Fuller test are employed to examine the cointegration among the markets. The hypothesis of no cointegration between India and other international stock market is rejected for all the stock price index using cross correlation test. But the Engle Granger ADF test provides sufficient evidence that there is no cointegration among India and other international stock markets. On the basis of the Granger causality test it is confirmed that the investors can enjoy the benefits of portfolio diversification in investing money in India.

References

1. Khan Masood Ahmad, Shahid Ashraf and Shahid Ahmed, "An Empirical Investigation of Causality and Dynamic Linkages: A case of Indian and American Equity Markets", **Prajnan**, Vol.33, No 3, 2005, pp.219–241.
2. Golaka, C. Nath and Sunil Verma, "Study of Common Trend and Integration in the Emerging stock–A Case Study of India, Singapore and Taiwan", **NSE News**, July 2003, pp.6–12.
3. Nalini Prava Tripathy, "Dynamic Relationship between Emerging Market and Developed Market: An Empirical Study in the Global Context", **The ICFAI journal of Applied Finance**, December 2005, p.49.
4. Grubel, H., "International Diversified Portfolios: Welfare Gains and Capital Flows", **American Economic Reviews**, Vol.58, No.5, 1968, pp.1299–1314.
5. Deepak Chawla, P.K. Mohanty and Sameer Bhardwaj; "Random Walk Hypothesis and Integration among the Indian Stock Market Vis–a–Vis Some Developed Markets", **Prajnan,** Vol 34, No.2, 2005, p.114.
6. Maladonado, R., and S. Saunders, "International Portfolio Diversification and the Intertemporal Stability of International Stock Market Relationship, 1957-78", **Financial Management**, 1981, pp.54–63.
7. Philippatos, G.C., A. Christofi and P. Christofi, "The Intertemporal Stability of International Stock Market Relationships: Another View", **Financial Management,** 1983, pp.63–69.

8. Schollhammer, H., and O. Sand, "The Interdependence among the Stock Markets of Major European Countries and the United States: An Empirical Investigation of Interrelationships among National Stock Price Movements", **Management International Review**, 1985, pp.17–26.

9. Bennett, P., and J. Kelleher, "The International Transmission of Stock Price Disruption in October 1987", **Federal Reserve Bank of New York Quarterly Review**, Vol.13, 1988, pp.17–33.

10. Goodhart, C.A.E., "The International Transmission of Asset Price Volatility, Financial Market Volatility", **Federal Reserve Bank of Kansas City**, 1988, pp.79–121.

11. Eun, C.S., and S. Shim., "International Transmission of Stock Market Movements", **Journal of Financial and Quantitative Analysis**, Vol.24, No.2, 1989, pp.241–256.

12. Furstenberg, G. M., and B. N. Jeon, "International Stock Price Movements: Links and Messages", **Brookings Papers on Economic Activity**, Vol.1, 1989, pp.125–167.

13. Becker, K.G., J.E. Finnerty and M. Gupta, "The Intertemporal Relationship between the US and Japanese Stock Markets", **The Journal of Finance**, Vol.45, No.4, 1990, pp.1297–1305.

14. King, M.A., and S. Wadhwani, "Transmission of Volatility between Stock Markets", **Review of Financial Studies**, Vol.3, 1990, pp.5–33.

15. Malliaris, A.G., and J.L. Urrutia, "The International Crash of October 1987: Causality Tests", **Journal of Financial and Quantitative Analysis**, Vol.27, No.3, 1992, pp.353–364.

16. Hassan, M.K., and A. Naka, "Short Run and Long Run Dynamic Linkages among International Stock Markets", **International Review of Economics and Finance**, Vol.5, No.4, 1996, pp.387–405.

17. Baig, T., and I. Goldfjan, "Financial Market Contagion in Asian Crisis", **IMF Staff Papers**, Vol.46, 1999, pp.167–195.

18. Kumar, M., J.A. Chan-Lau, A. Richards and T. Sloek, "Turbulence in Global Stock Markets: Trends and Correlations", **International Monetary Fund**, 2001.

19. Granger, C., and O. Morgenstern, "Predictability of Stock Market Prices", MA, Lexington, 1970.

20. Agmon, T., "The Relations among Equity Markets in the United States, United Kingdom, Germany and Japan", **The Journal of Finance**, Vol.27, No.4, 1974, pp.839–855.

21. Branch, B., "Common Stock Performance and Inflation: An International Comparison", **The Journal of Business**, Vol.47, No.1, 1974, pp.48–52.

Chapter 7

Summary of Findings, Suggestions and Conclusion

7.1 Introduction

The growth of an economy is largely influenced by financial markets—they allocate financial resources that are mobilised from savers and investors among users in the economy. The stock market is witnessing its function in the development of the country and is increasingly gaining importance. The Indian stock exchanges have captured prominent place not only in Asia but also on at the global stage. The globalization of economic activity, the increased world wealth, and the reduction in transaction costs associated with the information revolution direct all the investors to consider the newly emerging financial markets. Interaction of financial markets is one of the most extensively discussed topics of financial literature. So this study is aimed to understand the dynamic inter-linkages between Indian stock exchange and the stock exchanges of developing and developed countries.

In this context, the present study has been undertaken to analyse the following aspects.

- ☆ To test the weak form of Market efficiency of the stock markets of India and International Stock Markets.
- ☆ To determine the volatility levels in the stock markets of India and International Stock Markets.
- ☆ To draw a comparison between the Stock Markets of India and International Stock Markets important parameters like market capitalization, GDP, return and Volatility.
- ☆ To examine cointegrationa and causality among Indian and International Markets.

7.2 Data

The empirical work is based on daily closing prices of the stock indices. Only secondary data were used. The data consisted of daily series of the S and P CNX Nifty (India), NASDAQ (USA), Nikkei (Japan), Hang–Seng (Hong Kong), TW11 (Taiwan) and STI (Singapore). Shanghai Composite (China) Jakarta Composite (Indonesia) KLSE Composite (Malaysia) Seoul Composite (South Korea) Australia (AORD), FTSE (UK), Dax(France) and CAC 40 (Germany). The data on daily stock markets indices were downloaded from the Yahoo Finance website (http://finance.yahoo.com).

7.3 Summary of Findings

7.3.1 Features and Characteristics of the Various Stock Markets

The Stock Exchange in India

In India market capitalization was very low in the year 2001 because of dot.com problem. The total market capitalisation was very high in the year 2007 (1,819,100 $US million). As on 31st March 2012 the total market capitalisation was $ US 12, 63, 335 Million.

The Stock Exchange in Indonesia

In Indonesia there was a steady growth in market capitalization from 2000–2007 but in 2008 its market capitalization was very low because of global financial crisis. As end of 2012, the Indonesia Stock Exchange had 462 listed companies with a combined market capitalisation of US $ 39,67,721 billion.

The Stock Exchange in Malaysia

Malaysian stock market capitalization was steadily increasing from 2000 to 2007. In 2008 it tumbled down due to global financial crisis afterwards the market rebounded.

The Stock Exchange in Korea

South Korea's export focused economy was hit hard by the 2008 global economic downturn, but quickly rebounded in subsequent years, reaching over 6 per cent growth in 2010. The US-Korea Free Trade Agreement was ratified by both governments in 2011 and went into effect in March 2012.

Stock Exchange in China

In 2010 China became the world's largest exporter. Reforms began with the phasing out of collectivized agriculture, and expanded to include the gradual liberalization of prices, fiscal decentralization, increased autonomy for state enterprises, growth of the private sector, development of stock markets and a modern banking system, and opening to foreign trade and investment. The government's 12th Five-Year Plan, adopted in March 2011, emphasized continued economic reforms and the need to increase domestic consumption in order to make the economy less dependent in the future on fixed investments, exports, and heavy industry.

Stock Exchange in Taiwan

Taiwan has a dynamic capitalist economy with gradually decreasing government guidance of investment and foreign trade. Exports, led by electronics, machinery, and petrochemicals have provided the primary impetus for economic development. This heavy dependence on exports exposes the economy to fluctuations in world demand. Taiwan's diplomatic isolation, low birth rate, and rapidly aging population are other major long-term challenges.

The Stock Exchange in Australia

Australia plays an active role in the World Trade Organization, APEC, the G20, and other trade forums. Australia continues to negotiate bilateral agreements with India and Indonesia, as well as larger agreements with its Pacific neighbors and the Gulf Cooperation Council countries, and an Asia-wide Regional Comprehensive Economic Partnership that includes the ten ASEAN countries and China, Japan, Korea, New Zealand and India.

The Stock Exchange in Singapore

Singapore has a highly developed and successful free-market economy. It enjoys a remarkably open and corruption-free environment, stable prices, and a per capita GDP higher than that of most developed countries. The economy contracted 0.6 per cent in 2009 as a result of the global financial crisis, but has continued to grow since 2010 on the strength of renewed exports.

The Stock Exchange in Japan

While self-sufficient in rice production, Japan imports about 60 per cent of its food on a caloric basis. Modest economic growth continued after 2000, but the economy has fallen into recession four times since 2008.

The Stock Exchange in France

The French economy is diversified across all sectors. The government has partially or fully privatized many large companies, including Air France, France Telecom, Renault, and Thales. The budget deficit rose sharply from 3.3 per cent of GDP in 2008 to 7.5 per cent of GDP in 2009. Market capitalisation was very high in 2007.

The Stock Exchange in Germany

Market capitalization reached its peak in the year 2007. Following the March 2011 Fukushima nuclear disaster, has plummeted the market.

The Stock Exchange in Hong Kong

Hong Kong has a free market economy, highly dependent on international trade and finance - the value of goods and services trade, including the sizable share of re-exports, is about four times GDP. Hong Kong's open economy left it exposed to the global economic slowdown that began in 2008. Market capitalization was again low in the year 2011.

The Stock Exchange in US

The US has the most technologically powerful economy in the world, with a per capita GDP of $54,800. The sub-prime mortgage crisis, falling home prices, investment bank failures, tight credit, and the global economic downturn pushed the United States into a recession by mid-2008.

The Stock Exchange in London

In UK following the 2008-09 global economic crisis, the EU economy saw moderate GDP growth in 2010 and 2011 but has struggled since the sovereign debt crisis in the euro zone intensified in 2011.

7.3.2 Analysis of GDP Growth Trend

The entire Capital market segment has experienced both linear and compound growth trend. All the countries experienced linear and compound tren in the GDP growth. The behavior of stock prices in the developed and the emerging stock markets are analysed. The daily returns of stock price are examined. The traditional test namely Kolmogorov Smirnov Goodness of Fit Test (K-S test) runs test, autocorrelation test, Ljung Box test and the dynamic test the Augmented Dickey Fuller test and Philip Peron test are employed to examine the efficiency of the market. The hypothesis of the randomness of the stock returns are rejected for stock price index changes at all frequencies using Kolmogorov Smirnov Goodness of Fit Test (K-S test), Run Test auto correlation test and Ljung Box test. The rejection of null hypothesis indicates that the market is not weak form efficient. But the unit root hypothesis provides sufficient evidence that stock prices of all the stock markets follow random walk process. The results of the non-stationary variables support random walk hypothesis. On the basis of the unit root test (nonstationarity) it is confirmed that all stock markets are weak form efficient.

7.3.3 Return and Volatility

Yearwise Returns

The descriptive statistics were used to know the properties of the series. Among all the markets Indonesia earned highest income (0.0680) and India earned (0.0413) in the long run. Emerging markets performed better than developed markets. Except Taiwan all the emerging markets earned return in the long run. Indonesia and India performed better than the rest of the emerging markets and many of the major markets. Among developed markets Australia Singapore and Hong Kong all the other markets suffered loss in the long run.

Yearwise Volatility

In India, open to open and close to close volatility appears to be neck to neck. In the developed countries except Australia interlay volatility was very low in the year 2005 2006. It clearly exhibits that developed countries moved in tandem with each other. USA scored higher volatility compared to all the developed markets. Intra-day and inter -day movements in stock prices are considerably stable in Australia. Inter -day volatility has been consistently lower than 1 per cent and even the high and low price movement variation is also low.

Among all the emerging markets the intra-day volatility was very high in India and China in the year 2008-09. The developed markets UK, Hong-Kong, Singapore; Japan and emerging markets Kola Lumpur, Korea, Taiwan and India moved in tandem.

7.3.4 Dynamic Linkages between India and other International Stock Markets

During the pre crisis period there was a unidirectional Granger causality running from India to Indonesia, Kola Lumpur, Taiwan, Japan, Hong Kong and Germany. Bidirectional Granger causality exists between India and Korea, Australia and Singapore. During the post crisis period there was a unidirectional Granger causality running from India to China, Kola Lumpur, Korea, Taiwan, Australia, Japan and Hong Kong and unidirectional Granger causality running from Singapore, France, and US to India. Bidirectional Granger causality exists between India and Indonesia, India and Germany and India and UK during the post crisis period.

The direction of causality is also checked by using cross – correlations on returns. The results of cross – correlation test are presented in the Table 6.8 to 6.16. The cross – correlation test re- confirm results of Granger – causality test. There is no such significant difference between the markets before and after the financial crisis except Japan. The cross relation between India and Japan is very high after crisis. There is no cross relation between India and Germany and US after the crisis.

The results show evidence of weaker cross correlations among India and European, UK and US stock markets. Hence it can be said that the Indian markets offer diversification benefits to international investors looking for investment in India

7.4 Conclusion

Areas for further research

Performance analysis of NSE and BSE.

Market efficiency of NSE and BSE.

Volatility of stock price movements in BSE and NSE.

Cointegration among NSE and the developed stock markets.

www.ingramcontent.com/pod-product-compliance
Ingram Content Group UK Ltd.
Pitfield, Milton Keynes, MK11 3LW, UK
UKHW022210051026
15624UKWH00001B/92

9 789389 605204